ETERNAL SECURITY

Jacob Higgs

ISBN 979-8-89526-254-2 (paperback)
ISBN 979-8-89526-255-9 (digital)

Christian Faith Publishing
832 Park Avenue
Meadville, PA 16335
www.christianfaithpublishing.com

Printed in the United States of America

CONTENTS

OPENING

THEY SHALL NEVER PERISH. (John 10:27–30)

The ETERNAL SECURITY of HIS SHEEP

> My sheep hear my voice, and I know them, and they follow me:
> And I give unto them eternal life; and they shall never perish, neither shall any man pluck them out of my hand.
> My Father, which gave them me, is greater than all; and no man is able to pluck them out of my Father's hand.
> I and my Father are one. (John 10:27–30)

The question about the nature of biblical salvation and whether or not a believing sinner can get saved and be eternally secure or not is one of the most interesting and important subjects that can be researched in the Bible. It is certainly a source of great debate, with good men coming down on both sides of the discussion: some affirming that if a person ever does get genuinely saved, he or she will continue to possess that salvation forever, while others believe that one can indeed be saved at a certain point in life but later lose possession of that salvation because of subsequent choices and actions.

This will be the topic of this study, and it is my hope and prayer that you will approach this study as did the BEREANS, who were commended by our Lord in the book of Acts in chapter 17.

> And the brethren immediately sent away Paul and Silas by night unto Berea: who coming thither went into the synagogue of the Jews.
>
> These were more noble than those in Thessalonica, in that they received the word with all readiness of mind, and searched the scriptures daily, whether those things were so.
>
> Therefore many of them believed; also of honourable women which were Greeks, and of men, not a few. (Acts 17:10–12)

There is great nobility in approaching the Bible with an open mind and in letting it speak for itself without preconceived notions that can get in the way of our coming to the "rightly divided," "straight and narrow" conclusions that are in accordance with the "whole counsel of God."

Rightly divided

The properly balanced understanding of the overall tenor of the Scriptures' teaching on a particular subject. The individual who can do this understands that there are many individual verses that can be taken out of the Bible's overall context to steer a person a little left of center or right of center by themselves from the center line of truth.

> Study to shew thyself approved unto God, a workman that needeth not to be ashamed, rightly dividing the word of truth. (2 Timothy 2:15)

Straight and narrow

The Bible portrays the path that God wants us to follow, as revealed in His Word, as a straight and narrow path. When one turns to the right or the left to walk outside of this path or to think outside the lines—to use a contemporary phrase—of His Word, he or she is not walking or thinking correctly and must turn back to conform to God's ways and thoughts.

> Enter ye in at the strait gate: for wide is the gate, and broad is the way, that leadeth to destruc- tion, and many there be which go in thereat:
> Because strait is the gate, and narrow is the way, which leadeth unto life, and few there be that find it. (Matthew 7:13–14)

> And thine ears shall hear a word behind thee, saying, This is the way, walk ye in it, when ye turn to the right hand, and when ye turn to the left. (Isaiah 30:21)

> Casting down imaginations, and every high thing that exalteth itself against the knowledge of God, and bringing into captivity every thought to the obedience of Christ. (2 Corinthians 10:5)

Whole Counsel of God: This phrase refers to the entirety of the revelation of God to man as opposed to certain parts, verses, or segments. This takes into consideration everything from Genesis 1:1 all the way through Revelation 22:21.

> For I have not shunned to declare unto you all the counsel of God. (Acts 20:27)

CHAPTER 1

Framing the Questions of the
Debate on Eternal Security

As we begin our journey into the subject of eternal security and whether or not the Bible teaches the doctrine, there are several important questions that should typically be considered.

1. What IS the doctrine of eternal security?

Answer: The doctrine of eternal security is a theological (the study of God) title given to a teaching in the Bible that states that if a person ever truly gets SAVED from God's condemnation FOR sin and the consequent penalty and punishment in hell and the lake of fire, then that individual can NEVER LOSE that salvation and COME BACK UNDER God's condemnation for sin with its consequent penalty and punishment in hell and the lake of fire.

> Verily, verily, I say unto you, He that heareth my word, and believeth on him that sent me, hath everlasting life, and shall not come into condemnation; but is passed from death unto life. (John 5:24)

In other words, this doctrine asserts that once a man is genuinely saved in accordance with the scriptural definition of that term, he can never lose it but is eternally secure forever. This doctrine states that salvation is given to a man by God as a COVENANTAL GIFT while he is yet living and that God will never take it back from man or break His covenant (agreement with man) forever.

2. Does the Bible teach the doctrine of eternal security?

It is without a single doubt the conclusion of this pastor that the Bible DOES, in fact, definitely teach the doctrine of eternal security. Examine these things with an open mind, and then search the Scriptures daily to see for yourself and come to your own conclusion based on the weight of the evidence set before you.

3. Does the doctrine of eternal security allow for a person to get saved and then to "live like the devil" and do whatever he wants and to still be saved?

That question represents the fundamental misunderstanding that is really at the very heart of the debate. It reflects a multifaceted misunderstanding of the nature of salvation, and I will seek to address some of those misconceptions within this study. Please allow me to briefly point out here just a couple of the main points that will be elaborated on further in subsequent pages.

a. Salvation is NOT BASED UPON man's WORKS, what we DO—neither in its acquisition nor in its continuation—so the question really reveals that, on some level, the person asking it BELIEVES that a man's works do have something to do with his obtaining or maintaining his salvation. God says that it is "not by works of righteousness, which we have done, but according to His mercy He saved us, by the washing of regeneration and renewing of the Holy Ghost" in Titus 3:5.

b. Salvation IS BASED UPON GRACE THROUGH FAITH—NOT WORKS—according to Ephesians 2:8–9, and the grace of God that brings salvation TEACHES US SEVERAL THINGS that fly in the face of the idea that a true child of God has any business "living like the devil and doing whatever he wants." Read it for yourself in Titus 2:11–15.

> For the grace of God that bringeth salvation hath appeared to all men,
> Teaching us that, denying ungodliness and worldly lusts, we should live soberly, righteously, and godly, in this present world;
> Looking for that blessed hope, and the glorious appearing of the great God and our Saviour Jesus Christ;
> Who gave himself for us, that he might redeem us from all iniquity, and purify unto himself a peculiar people, zealous of good works.
> These things speak, and exhort, and rebuke with all authority. Let no man despise thee. (Titus 2:11–15)

The grace of God that saves takes us into the classroom and says, "Sit down, class, we have a lot to cover before you go home!" God has expectations for His children. You SAY you are saved; don't go around living like the devil. You are to live soberly, righteously, and godly in this present world. You are to live a pure life that is peculiar unto others and on fire to do good works for God—NOT TO SAVE YOU BUT BECAUSE YOU ARE SAVED!

When someone asks that question, they are revealing a fundamental misunderstanding of the basis for salvation and manifesting that their hope of heaven is at least partially resting upon their own WORKS and NOT ONLY AND ENTIRELY UPON THE WORK OF CHRIST ALONE! However, God affirms that a man is SAVED BY FAITH AND KEPT BY FAITH (Ephesians 2:8–9; compare with the statement in 1 Peter 1:5)—NOT BY WORKS.

A definition of works

For the purpose of our discussion here on the subject of biblical salvation, I am going to define the word *WORKS* as referring to any action or activity, whether entered into actively or passively, that someone might view as being a reasonable basis for obtaining the forgiveness and favor of God. When I say that I am referring to any action or activity, whether entered into actively or passively, I am talking about the difference between an action, which would involve taking initiative, and personal action like doing a good deed of some kind or giving money to a religious organization, and a passive activity, which might include something like being baptized or receiving communion. Unfortunately, many sincere people in the world today have been led to believe that their ACTIONS have some part in their acquiring and (or) keeping their salvation, and nothing could be more unscriptural.

> For by grace are ye saved through faith; and that not of yourselves: it is the gift of God:
> Not of works, lest any man should boast.
> For we are his workmanship, created in Christ Jesus unto good works, which God hath before ordained that we should walk in them. (Ephesians 2:8–10)

> Who are kept by the power of God through faith unto salvation ready to be revealed in the last time. (1 Peter 1:5)

> Not by works of righteousness which we have done, but according to his mercy he saved us, by the washing of regeneration, and renewing of the Holy Ghost;
> Which he shed on us abundantly through Jesus Christ our Saviour;

That being justified by his grace, we should be made heirs according to the hope of eternal life.

This is a faithful saying, and these things I will that thou affirm constantly, that they which have believed in God might be careful to maintain good works. These things are good and profitable unto men. (Titus 3:5–8)

As you can see from the Holy Spirit's instructions in Titus 3, good works do not PRODUCE salvation as a prerequisite, but they are definitely to FOLLOW our salvation as a PRODUCT OF OUR SAVING FAITH. I will have more to say on that later.

The great question is, WHAT DOES ONE BELIEVE with regard to how he hopes to go to Heaven when he dies? If his actions enter at all into the equation, his faith is not resting solely upon the finished work of Jesus Christ ALONE as his only hope of heaven. If that is the case, the individual must repent of his misplaced faith (the portion that is resting upon what HE DOES), and he MUST place it ALL ON JESUS ALONE AND HIS FINISHED WORK!

c. Because salvation is not acquired by works and is not kept by works, it is possible for a saved person to sin after his salvation and not lose his salvation thereby. However, the Bible certainly does not encourage the idea that a man can get saved and live as he wants to live. Furthermore, the Bible clearly states that the joy of one's salvation can be forfeited for a time when one sins after salvation, even though his soul remains saved. This can be seen in the life of David after his sin with Bathsheba in the Old Testament, especially in Psalm 51:12. It also teaches that cleansing can be received and joy can be restored if one will honestly confess his sin to God and ask, as is seen in Psalm 51 and in 1 John 1:9.

4. If the Bible does teach the doctrine of eternal security for the believer, then why are there so many verses that contradict that idea?

The simple answer to that question is that there are no verses that actually contradict that teaching, but there are some that can certainly SEEM to do so if they are not examined within the context of the "whole counsel of God." I will spend a good amount of time later in this study carefully examining several of those questionable passages and attempting to help you understand them within that overall context mentioned above.

CHAPTER 2

The Basis for Biblical Salvation

NOTE: Before a person can understand the doctrine of eternal security as it relates to the salvation of a soul, one must first understand the reason salvation is needed, how it was provided for man by God, and how it is appropriated by man.

A. The HOLINESS of God and the PURITY of heaven are why salvation is NEEDED by man (2 Peter 1:15–16 and Revelation 21:27).

God is ABSOLUTELY HOLY in nature and conduct. Stop and think about that for a moment! God is ABSOLUTELY HOLY in His nature (who and what He is) and in His conduct (what HE DOES).

> But as he which hath called you is holy, so
> be ye holy in all manner of conversation;
> Because it is written, Be ye holy; for I am
> holy. (1 Peter 1:15–16)

Heaven is an ABSOLUTELY 100 percent pure place, and God has decided that He will not allow ANYTHING into heaven that would defile it or make it unclean in any way, even to the tiniest degree.

> And there shall in no wise enter into it any thing that defileth, neither whatsoever worketh abomination, or maketh a lie: but they which are written in the Lamb's book of life. (Revelation 21:27)

Now take a moment to really THINK about THAT. A sanitary environment is very important when a doctor is performing surgery, and even a few germs can be totally unacceptable if you are a doctor who cares about his patients. Germs breed infections, and infections can kill. Our world is terribly infected with sin and the death and destruction that it brings, but Almighty God has a wonderful place that He has preserved and will preserve from the awful *germ* of sin. God doesn't refuse men home in heaven because He is unloving OR because He likes to send men to hell and the lake of fire to suffer forever. He simply CANNOT ALLOW the germ of sin to enter into heaven and defile His wonderful house with death and destruction. Heaven is the one safe haven from the defilement of sin!

B. The CONDITION of man in the sight of god makes salvation a necessity for every man.

1. THERE IS NONE RIGHTEOUS OR PROFITABLE TO GOD.

> As it is **written**, There is none righteous, no, not one:
> There is none that understandeth, there is none that seeketh after God. (Romans 3:10)

> They are all gone out of the way, they are together become unprofitable; there is none that doeth good, no, not one. (Romans 3:12)

2. ALL MEN ARE SINNERS WHO HAVE COME SHORT OF HIS
    GLORY. His standard of perfect holiness.

    For all have sinned, and come short of the
    glory of God. (Romans 3:23)

3. ALL MEN HAVE GONE ASTRAY FROM GOD and ARE
    SELF-SERVING.

    All we like sheep have gone astray; we have
    turned every one to his own way; and the LORD
    hath laid on him the iniquity of us all. (Isaiah
    53:6)

4. ALL OF OUR GOOD DEEDS ARE UNCLEAN IN HIS SIGHT
    BECAUSE WE ARE UNCLEAN, SO WE CANNOT SAVE OURSELVES.

    But we are all as an unclean thing, and all
    our righteousnesses are as filthy rags; and we all
    do fade as a leaf; and our iniquities, like the wind,
    have taken us away. (Isaiah 64:6)

C. The SEPARATION of man from God and heaven because of
    sin necessitates that a man be saved.

    Behold, the LORD's hand is not shortened,
    that it cannot save; neither his ear heavy, that it
    cannot hear:
    But your Iniquities have Separated between
    you and your God, and your sins have hid his face
    from you, that he will not hear. (Isaiah 59:1–2)

    And there shall in no wise enter into it any
    thing that defileth, neither whatsoever worketh
    abomination, or maketh a lie: but they which are

written in the Lamb's book of life. (Revelation 21:27)

Behold, all souls are mine; as the soul of the father, so also the soul of the son is mine: the soul that sinneth, it shall die. (Ezekiel 18:4)

And I saw a great white throne, and him that sat on it, from whose face the earth and the heaven fled away; and there was found no place for them.

And I saw the dead, small and great, stand before God; and the books were opened: and another book was opened, which is the book of life: and the dead were judged out of those things which were written in the books, according to their works.

And the sea gave up the dead which were in it; and death and hell delivered up the dead which were in them: and they were judged every man according to their works.

And death and hell were cast into the lake of fire. This is the second death.

And whosoever was not found written in the book of life was cast into the lake of fire. (Revelation 20:11–15)

Note: Sin brings uncleanness and defilement, which God cannot allow into heaven.

It is because of this that all of mankind needs a Savior. If a man dies "in his sins," he must be separated from God and heaven and go to the lake of fire forever. This is because, though God loves man very much, He cannot allow the defilement of sin into His holy dwelling place. This is very understandable for any mother who has told her little boy that he will not be allowed into the house to walk on Mama's freshly mopped kitchen floor until he takes off his muddy shoes. She doesn't hate the boy; she just wants to keep her clean house clean.

Good deeds can never gain us entrance into heaven because we are spiritually unclean before God from sins. The Bible says that all of our righteousnesses are as filthy rags, which means that the good things we do are not acceptable to God because we offer them to Him with dirty hands. Good deeds cannot take away the stain of our sins. It is like a doctor performing surgery with dirty hands. The surgeon may be willing to perform the surgery for no money at all, but the germs on his hands make him unacceptable as a surgeon. You would say, "No thanks, Doc. I can't accept your offer." The only way that God will allow us into heaven is by washing away our sins in the precious blood of His dear Son, Jesus Christ, and that brings us to the next major point.

D.   God's ANSWER for man's sin and separation

Jesus PAID the PENALTY for our sins on the cross and offered His own precious blood to wash our sins away and BRING US BACK to God.

> For the wages of sin is death; but the gift of
> God is eternal life through Jesus Christ our Lord.
> (Romans 6:23)

> But God commendeth his love toward us,
> in that, while we were yet sinners, Christ died
> for us.
> Much more then, being now justified by
> his blood, we shall be saved from wrath through
> him. (Romans 5:8)

> For Christ also hath once suffered for sins,
> the just for the unjust, that he might bring us to
> God, being put to death in the flesh, but quick-
> ened by the Spirit. (1 Peter 3:18)

Who his own self bare our sins in his own body on the tree, that we, being dead to sins, should live unto righteousness: by whose stripes ye were healed.

For ye were as sheep going astray; but are now returned unto the Shepherd and Bishop of your souls. (1 Peter 2:24–25)

For if the blood of bulls and of goats, and the ashes of an heifer sprinkling the unclean, sanctifieth to the purifying of the flesh:

How much more shall the blood of Christ, who through the eternal Spirit offered himself without spot to God, purge your conscience from dead works to serve the living God?

And for this cause he is the mediator of the new testament, that by means of death, for the redemption of the transgressions that were under the first testament, they which are called might receive the promise of eternal inheritance.

For where a testament is, there must also of necessity be the death of the testator.

For a testament is of force after men are dead: otherwise it is of no strength at all while the testator liveth.

Whereupon neither the first testament was dedicated without blood.

For when Moses had spoken every precept to all the people according to the law, he took the blood of calves and of goats, with water, and scarlet wool, and hyssop, and sprinkled both the book, and all the people,

Saying, This is the blood of the testament which God hath enjoined unto you.

Moreover he sprinkled with blood both the tabernacle, and all the vessels of the ministry.

And almost all things are by the law purged with blood; and without shedding of blood is no remission.

It was therefore necessary that the patterns of things in the heavens should be purified with these; but the heavenly things themselves with better sacrifices than these.

For Christ is not entered into the holy places made with hands, which are the figures of the true; but into heaven itself, now to appear in the presence of God for us.

Nor yet that he should offer himself often, as the high priest entereth into the holy place every year with blood of others;

For then must he often have suffered since the foundation of the world: but now once in the end of the world hath he appeared to put away sin by the sacrifice of himself.

And as it is appointed unto men once to die, but after this the judgment:

So Christ was once offered to bear the sins of many; and unto them that look for him shall he appear the second time without sin unto salvation. (Hebrews 9:13–28)

And the blood of Jesus Christ his Son cleanseth us from all sin. (1 John 1:7)

Now, friends, there is no salvation by doing good deeds because doing good deeds cannot wash away sin. It is also not by participating in sacred rituals or any works of righteousness because works and rituals performed by men CANNOT wash away the stain of our sins.

THAT IS WHY Jesus came to shed His precious blood and die on the cross. NOTICE: JESUS OFFERED ONE SACRIFICE FOR ALL SINS FOREVER!

For the law having a shadow of good things to come, and not the very image of the things, can never with those sacrifices which they offered year by year continually make the comers thereunto perfect.

For then would they not have ceased to be offered? Because that the worshippers once purged should have had no more conscience of sins.

But in those sacrifices there is a remembrance again made of sins every year.

For it is not possible that the blood of bulls and of goats should take away sins.

Wherefore when he cometh into the world, he saith, Sacrifice and offering thou wouldest not, but a body hast thou prepared me:

In burnt offerings and sacrifices for sin Thou hast had no pleasure.

Then said I, Lo, I come (in the volume of the book it is written of Me,) to do thy will, O God.

Above when he said, Sacrifice and offering and burnt offerings and offering for sin thou wouldest not, neither hadst pleasure therein; which are offered by the law;

Then said he, Lo, I come to do thy will, O God. He taketh away the first, that he may establish the second.

By the which will we are sanctified through the offering of the body of Jesus Christ ONCE for ALL.

And every priest standeth daily ministering and offering oftentimes the same sacrifices, which can never take away sins:

But this man, after he had offered one sacrifice for sins for ever, sat down on the right hand of God;

From henceforth expecting till his enemies be made his footstool.

For by ONE Offering he hath perfected for ever them that are sanctified.

Whereof the Holy Ghost also is a witness to us: for after that He had said before,

This is the covenant that I will make with them after those days, saith the Lord, I will put my laws into their hearts, and in their minds will I write them;

And their sins and iniquities will I remember no more.

Now where remission of these is, there is no more offering for sin.

Having therefore, brethren, boldness to enter into the holiest by the blood of Jesus,

By a new and living way, which he hath consecrated for us, through the veil, that is to say, his flesh;

And having an high priest over the house of God;

Let us draw near with a true heart in full assurance of faith, having our hearts sprinkled from an evil conscience, and our bodies washed with pure water.

Let us hold fast the profession of our faith without wavering; (for he is faithful that promised;)

And let us consider one another to provoke unto love and to good works:

Not forsaking the assembling of ourselves together, as the manner of some is; but exhorting one another: and so much the more, as ye see the day approaching.

> For if we sin willfully after that we have received the knowledge of the truth, there remaineth no more sacrifice for sins,
>
> But a certain fearful looking for of judgment and fiery indignation, which shall devour the adversaries.
>
> He that despised Moses' law died without mercy under two or three witnesses:
>
> Of how much sorer punishment, suppose ye, shall he be thought worthy, who hath trodden under foot the Son of God, and hath counted the blood of the covenant, wherewith he was sanctified, an unholy thing, and hath done despite unto the Spirit of grace? (Hebrews 10:1–29)

WHY IS SALVATION ETERNAL?

WHY IS IT IMPOSSIBLE TO LOSE SALVATION IF A PERSON EVER ACTUALLY HAS IT?

READ HEBREWS 10:14 AGAIN.

> For by one offering He hath perfected forever them that are sanctified. (Hebrews 10:14)

The blood of Jesus Christ spiritually cleanses and sanctifies the believing sinner forever, and it is the ONLY thing that can. Notice, it is Christ who perfects the sinner, not the sinner perfecting himself (by works or ritual sacrifices). The perfection is by the means of His ONE offering for sin. The perfecting and sanctification Christ provides is forever.

One thing that may help you understand eternal security is to remember that salvation is an EVENT, NOT A PROCESS! By that, we mean that a person is saved at a certain specific point in time in his or her life when he or she understands their sinful condition and how their sins will separate them from God and heaven forever unless they accept God's plan of salvation as revealed in the Scriptures. At that point in time, when people understand God's assessment of their sinful condition and their consequent separation, they must also know about God's answer to their problem through the sacrifice of His Son, who was offered on the cross as a one-time offering for sins to pay the wage of sin, which is death, and cleanse their souls from sin by His own blood forever.

Once people know about their sinful condition, their separation from God and heaven, and God's answer to their problem through the sacrifice of Jesus, they must take God's prescription to be saved. When they do, they enter an eternal covenant with God that secures their soul forever.

E. God's PRESCRIPTION for man to RECEIVE His SALVATION

a. God calls upon man to REPENT.

And the times of this ignorance God winked at; but now commandeth all men every where to repent:
Because he hath appointed a day, in the which he will judge the world in righteousness by that man whom he hath ordained; whereof he hath given assurance unto all men, in that he hath raised him from the dead. (Acts 17:30–31)

Seek ye the LORD while he may be found, call ye upon him while he is near:
Let the wicked forsake his way, and the unrighteous man his thoughts: and let him return unto the LORD, and he will have mercy upon him; and to our God, for he will abundantly pardon.
For my thoughts are not your thoughts, neither are your ways my ways, saith the LORD.
For as the heavens are higher than the earth, so are my ways higher than your ways, and my thoughts than your thoughts. (Isaiah 55:6–9)

b. God Calls Upon Man to RECEIVE HIS SON AS LORD and SAVIOUR.

And said unto them, Thus it is written, and thus it behoved Christ to suffer, and to rise from the dead the third day:

And that repentance and remission of sins should be preached in his name among all nations, beginning at Jerusalem. (Luke 24:46–47)

Testifying both to the Jews, and also to the Greeks, repentance toward God, and faith toward our Lord Jesus Christ. (Acts 20:21)

That if thou shalt confess with thy mouth the Lord Jesus, and shalt believe in thine heart that God hath raised him from the dead, thou shalt be saved. (Romans 10:9)

But as many as received him, to them gave he power to become the sons of God, even to them that believe on his name. (John 1:12)

IF YOU HAVE NEVER DONE SO, WE INVITE YOU TO PRAY THIS PRAYER WITH A SINCERE HEART:

Dear God, I know that I'm a sinner and that I've lived my life my own way. I admit that I've been wrong, and I'm sorry, God. I believe that Jesus died for my sins so I could be forgiven, and I ask for Your gift of salvation through Him. I repent of going my way, Lord, and I choose today to live for Jesus for the rest of my life because He died for me. Come into my heart, Lord Jesus. I receive YOU today as my ONLY HOPE of heaven. In Jesus's name, I pray, AMEN.

CHAPTER 3

Understanding the Twofold
Nature of Salvation

Luke 24:46–47
Mark 1:14–15
Acts 20:21
Hebrews 6:1

A. Salvation is both JUDICIAL and ATTITUDINAL.

What we mean by this statement is that salvation deals with both a man's judicial standing before God as a guilty sinner before his Creator and Judge, and also with his attitude of rebellion, like a sheep going astray to follow his own path AWAY from his shepherd.

Essentially, the message of the Gospel confronts man's sense of self-righteousness, points out his guilt and condemnation before God because of sin and its defilement, and points him to the sacrifice of Jesus as his only hope for forgiveness and going to Heaven when he dies.

The message of repentance addresses the mindset that justifies the idea that a man can live his life on his own terms based on what he thinks or feels is right for him, OR what he wants to do, regardless of what God says in the Bible, AND points him to JESUS, WHO IS THE WAY, and the WORD of God, and the Good Shepherd that man should RETURN to and FOLLOW.

B.   Most churches only address the judicial aspect of salvation.

Most churches, unfortunately, only focus on the Gospel, which deals with God's judgment and justice, but ignore the doctrine of repentance. Many liberal preachers avoid the doctrine of repentance because they know that they will lose their audience if they present them with any form of expectations that they don't want to hear. They would rather scratch the people's *itching ears* than tell them the truth at any cost.

Many conservative preachers also avoid the doctrine of repentance because they don't want to be guilty of preaching a *faith plus works Gospel.* This is very noble in a way, but it offers a false hope to many people who are unwilling to acknowledge their fundamental rebellion against the ways and thoughts of God, while at the same time claiming to love and follow Jesus, WHO IS THE WAY.

It is also based on the false assumption that somehow, when the change of mind (called repentance) is preached as being required before one can be truly saved, that somehow translates into a "faith plus works Gospel," which of course would be unbiblical. The main error here is mistaking the root of salvation with the fruit of salvation.

While conservative preachers clearly recognize that WORKS are the FRUIT of salvation and must NEVER be REQUIRED as PREREQUISITES for salvation, they often overlook the necessity of one's having the change of mind that is GIVEN BY GOD, AS IS SAVING FAITH IN THE GOSPEL, as being a prerequisite for one's salvation. The change of mind (repentance) about WHO is the WAY to heaven and WHAT is the WAY that is right for a man to live is the root of salvation that inevitably produces the fruit of a new life and new works. It is NOT BY works, though, that any man is saved (Titus 3:5; Ephesians 2:8–9).

C.   The reason many supposed Christians never bear fruit.

This is the reason many people who profess to be Christians think nothing of living lives that are totally opposed to the straight and narrow path laid out in the Bible and why they bring forth no "fruits worthy of repentance," as John the Baptist commanded in

Luke 3:7–8 and as Paul instructed in Acts 26:20. It is also why many walk away from God after professing faith.

> D. Repentance changes the way one looks at God, and self, and life itself forever.

If anyone finally recognizes and acknowledges that God's ways are higher than man's ways, that God's thoughts ARE higher than man's thoughts, AND that JESUS CHRIST IS THE WAY OF GOD, THEN the prospect of receiving Him as Lord and Savior and following Him for all eternity will immediately begin a new work that will change the direction of an individual's life forever. People need to understand that repentance deals with what a man BELIEVES is the right way and the best way to live his life. It is a fundamental change in a man's thinking, whereby he places MORE FAITH in THE WAY of God than he does in his own way of living.

Before a man is saved, he believes his own ways and thoughts are higher than God's, so he goes astray. Then God gives him repentance to the acknowledging of the TRUTH!

Repentance, like saving faith, is a GIFT from God. This can be seen by comparing Ephesians 2:8–9 and 2 Timothy 2:24–25. These two gifts are offered to man by God simultaneously through the Word of God, by the ministry of the Holy Spirit. In that wonderfully mysterious moment, when a man's heart receives the testimony of the Word of God and the Spirit of God, he is born again and becomes a new creature in Jesus Christ and possesses eternal life. From that time on, the man is no longer like a sheep going astray, but instead like one who has returned to his Good Shepherd and the Bishop of his soul, as Peter referred to in 1 Peter 2:25.

> For ye were as sheep going astray; but are
> now returned unto the Shepherd and Bishop of
> your souls. (1 Peter 2:25)

It has long been my contention that if anyone understands what Jesus meant in John 14:6 and sincerely believes it, then it makes no sense at all for that person to turn around and reject the authority of the Bible over his or her life. My contention is that when an individual says that they have received Jesus Christ as their Savior, but they stubbornly refuse to acknowledge and yield from the heart to His call for obedience, then they have believed in another Jesus and another Gospel than the ones presented in the Bible. Their prayer asking Jesus to come into their heart and be their Savior was an offering to God like Cain's was in the Scripture. This is what I have come to call Cain Christianity.

Note: This must not be construed as requiring sinless perfection OR saying that if a person has this mindset he will never have conflicting thoughts, feelings, or desires after receiving repentance. It also does not mean that a person who has genuinely repented will be incapable of falling into sin and yielding to temptation because though he has the mind of Christ (1 Corinthians 2:16), he is also living in a fleshly body, which is "sold under sin" (Romans 7:14), and he possesses at least the remnants of a "carnal mind," which is at enmity with God (Romans 8:7). This is why Paul talked about the inner conflict that rages inside a Christian because of these two contrary natures, lives, and laws battling for control within (Galatians 5:16–25; Romans 6–8). He also described the sense of self-loathing that takes place inside when a believer, who delights in the law of God in his inner man, yields to the law of sin, which is in the fleshly members of his body instead of walking after the Spirit of life and minding the promptings of the Holy Spirit.

THINK THIS THROUGH WITH ME NOW! Jesus IS the WORD OF GOD (John 1:1, 14). The BIBLE is the Word of God, given by divine inspiration (2 Timothy 3:16–17). Jesus IS THE TRUTH (John 14:6). God's Word is truth (John 17:17). Jesus IS THE WAY (John 14:6), so wouldn't the Bible be God's way?

If a Christian is a disciple or a follower of Jesus, shouldn't a Christian follow the Bible?

NOW PUT YOUR THINKING CAPS ON. ARE YOU READY? If people say they have received Jesus as the LIFE, can they still reject Him as the WAY? Can they reject the Bible as the WAY they should live? If a person rejects the Bible, God's Word, as his or her authority in life, is that person REALLY accepting Jesus (the WORD) as the bishop (overseer, boss, or ruler) of his or her soul as in 1 Peter 2:25?

Can a person accept Jesus as SAVIOR, but at the same time REJECT Him as LORD? Can a person reject Jesus as Lord and be saved anyway, just because he prayed a prayer? Does God save a sheep who is still determined to keep going his OWN WAY, ASTRAY FROM God? Or does the grace of God that brings salvation teach the wandering sheep that he must FORSAKE HIS OWN WAYS AND THOUGHTS AND RETURN to the shepherd to give heed to His voice and follow Him? Is THAT not the kind of person that Jesus identifies as being one of His sheep?

> My sheep hear my voice, and I know them,
> and they follow me:
> And I give unto them eternal life; and they
> shall never perish, neither shall any man pluck
> them out of my hand. (John 10:27–28)

Does not Isaiah characterize a lost soul as being a sheep going astray and having turned to His OWN WAY?

> All we like sheep have gone astray; we have
> turned every one to his own way; and the LORD
> hath laid on him the iniquity of us all. (Isaiah
> 53:6)

Doesn't Isaiah admonish the straying sheep to seek the Lord BY FORSAKING His own ways and thoughts and to RETURN to the Lord in order to receive mercy and pardon from God?

> Seek ye the LORD while he may be found,
> call ye upon him while he is near:
> Let the wicked forsake his way, and the
> unrighteous man his thoughts: and let him
> return unto the LORD, and he will have mercy

upon him; and to our God, for he will abundantly pardon. (Isaiah 55:6–7)

Doesn't God say through Isaiah that HIS WAYS AND THOUGHTS
ARE NOT THE SAME as man's, but that THEY ARE HIGHER THAN MAN'S
WAYS and thoughts?

> For my thoughts are not your thoughts, nei-
> ther are your ways my ways, saith the LORD.
> For as the heavens are higher than the earth,
> so are my ways higher than your ways, and my
> thoughts than your thoughts. (Isaiah 55:8–9)

Doesn't Peter, speaking to Christians, say that they had been like
sheep going astray but that they had RETURNED TO THE SHEPHERD
and bishop of their souls?

> For ye were as sheep going astray; but are
> now returned unto the Shepherd and Bishop of
> your souls. (1 Peter 2:25)

SOME PREACHERS MISTAKENLY BELIEVE THAT REPENTANCE IS
NOT A PREREQUISITE FOR SALVATION BUT THAT IS BECAUSE THEY
HAVE MISDEFINED THE CONCEPT.
They define repentance in such a way as to assert that if a person has genuinely repented, then that individual would no longer be
capable of sinning because he or she has changed his or her mind
about sin and has chosen God's ways over their own. I realize that I
changed the subject from singular to plural there, from HIS OR HER
to THEIR, but it makes sense because it applies to any number of people who might fall into that category. The aforementioned preachers also think the same way about the concept of lordship salvation.
They affirm that if an individual genuinely accepts Jesus Christ as
Lord, then he or she would never sin again; otherwise, Jesus would
not be Lord. What both of those misdefinitions fail to take into consideration is that what I call "shoe-leather obedience" always begins

with a decision of the heart to obey God's teachings because the mind has been changed with regard to the belief about whose ways and thoughts are, in fact, higher: God's or man's.

God has given repentance to the acknowledging of the truth that His ways are higher and nobler and that Jesus Christ IS Lord, whether a man will humble himself and acknowledge it or not. That teaching or doctrine is received and embraced at the heart level. However, every genuine Christian has a battle when it comes to working out what God is working into their lives. It does not mean that the sinner is no longer capable of sinning, but that his heart is no longer taking sides with and justifying the sin that dwells in his mortal body. He may certainly yield to its impulses and give in to its appetites, but at his heart level, he has a desire to DIE to THAT WAY OF LIFE that grieves the Holy Spirit. He no longer desires, at his deepest heart level, to live like a sheep going astray. He genuinely wants to hear and follow his Good Shepherd's voice. He is now, at a heart level, opposed to the idea that it does not matter what the Bible says. To this new man, the Bible is his highest ideal for life. He delights in the Word of God in his inner man. He wants to obey from the heart the doctrines it teaches.

However, because he is still living in a body that is sold under sin with carnal appetites and because he still has a carnal mind to deal with that is at enmity with God, he often finds himself struggling with the flesh lusting against the Spirit and the Spirit lusting against the flesh, pulling him in contrary directions. He may truly delight in the law of God in his inner man, but he sees another law (the law of sin) in his members (the fleshly parts of his body that are waiting to be changed into His body's glorious likeness), warring against the law of his mind and bringing him into captivity to the law of sin, even though he despises himself for every disgusting act of sin. Because how to perform that which is good he finds not. He confesses that Jesus Christ is Lord and has the most pure desire to obey from the heart but struggles with the process of sanctification and slowly learns through many defeats to walk in the Spirit and to walk after the Spirit. Genuine repentance is required for salvation.

However, genuine repentance does not automatically create perfect sinlessness.

In fact, the truth of the matter is that no man ever in this life arrives at a place of perfect sinlessness, but the WANTER in a man is transformed. A man's SPIRIT is born again by the incorruptible seed of the Word of God by the ministry of the Holy Spirit. That part of man is saved, sanctified, and seated with Jesus (at least in some spiritual capacity) in heavenly places.

Man's soul—his intellect, emotion, and will—is saved from the penalty of sin but is in a process of sanctification and is changed little by little as the law of the Lord converts the soul (the mind is brought into captivity to the obedience of the Word), and we are changed from glory to glory as we behold the face of Jesus, and we behold our own face through the Word by the ministry of the Holy Spirit.

During that process, we are subject to all of the struggles that Paul referred to in Romans 7:14–25. Our bodies are sold under sin and will not be fully sanctified until the Lord's return for us, whereupon He changes our vile bodies so that they may be fashioned like unto His glorious body. The spirit and soul of a Christian recognize and confess that Jesus Christ is LORD. The spirit cannot sin because it is already sanctified and seated, in a sense, with Jesus in heavenly places.

The soul is the battleground wherein sanctification is a work in progress. The body is enslaved to the sin principle and will remain so until the coming of the Lord, but IT CAN BE KEPT UNDER and brought into subjection by the power of the indwelling Spirit of God, as we learn to walk in and after His working in us both to will and to do of His good pleasure. The body cannot be completely subdued by just the choice of our will, as it will one day be by the Lord, who alone is able to subdue all things unto Himself.

Right now, the believer is in a crucible of sorts, to break out of the shell of our fleshly limitations, or at least to rise above their downward pull through the indwelling Spirit, much like a baby bird breaks out of his shell to soar in the skies on the wings of the wind.

It is the struggle that makes us strong and enables us to grow, survive, and eventually thrive in the gymnasium of the Lord (Ecclesiastes 3:10–11).

> I have seen the travail, which God hath given to the sons of men to be exercised in it.
>
> He hath made every thing beautiful in his time: also he hath set the world in their heart, so that no man can find out the work that God maketh from the beginning to the end. (Ecclesiastes 3:10–11)

> Wherefore, my beloved, as ye have always obeyed, not as in my presence only, but now much more in my absence, work out your own salvation with fear and trembling.
>
> For it is God which worketh in you both to will and to do of his good pleasure. (Philippians 2:12–13)

> For we know that the law is spiritual: but I am carnal, sold under sin.
>
> For that which I do I allow not: for what I would, that do I not; but what I hate, that do I.
>
> If then I do that which I would not, I consent unto the law that it is good.
>
> Now then it is no more I that do it, but sin that dwelleth in me.
>
> For I know that in me (that is, in my flesh,) dwelleth no good thing: for to will is present with me; but how to perform that which is good I find not.
>
> For the good that I would I do not: but the evil which I would not, that I do.
>
> Now if I do that I would not, it is no more I that do it, but sin that dwelleth in me.

I find then a law, that, when I would do good, evil is present with me.

For I delight in the law of God after the inward man:

But I see another law in my members, warring against the law of my mind, and bringing me into captivity to the law of sin which is in my members.

O wretched man that I am! who shall deliver me from the body of this death?

I thank God through Jesus Christ our Lord. So then with the mind I myself serve the law of God; but with the flesh the law of sin. (Romans 7:14–25)

There is therefore now no condemnation to them which are in Christ Jesus, who walk not after the flesh, but after the Spirit.

For the law of the Spirit of life in Christ Jesus hath made me free from the law of sin and death.

For what the law could not do, in that it was weak through the flesh, God sending his own Son in the likeness of sinful flesh, and for sin, condemned sin in the flesh:

That the righteousness of the law might be fulfilled in us, who walk not after the flesh, but after the Spirit. (Romans 8:1–4)

But if the Spirit of him that raised up Jesus from the dead dwell in you, he that raised up Christ from the dead shall also quicken your mortal bodies by his Spirit that dwelleth in you. (Romans 8:11)

The Holy Spirit is the wind under our wings. What we could not do (obey the law of God) through the flesh (it is the Spirit that quickeneth; the flesh profiteth nothing), God sent His Son in the likeness of sinful flesh and sentenced the flesh to death so that the Holy Spirit could come into us and quicken (enliven, give new life to) our mortal bodies and enable us to walk in newness of life by His power over death. Once these events have occurred, we have passed spiritually from death unto life, and nothing is able to separate us from the love of God in Christ. We are safe in His hands. He will in no wise cast us out, and no man (including ourselves) is ABLE to pluck us out of His hands (John 10:27–30). Our performance does not get us saved or keep us saved. We are utterly unable to perform that which is good without His help. Repentance changes our attitude about God from one of rebellion and faith in our own way and our determination to pursue our own path to one of faith in Him and His way and a determination to follow Him, who loved us and gave Himself for us. Our recognition of His lordship is the natural result of our change of mind and our receiving a love of the truth (2 Timothy 2:24–26; 2 Thessalonians 2:10–12).

Once this change in our thinking has occurred, we would never have any reason to turn back and walk away from God because we would be as convinced as Peter was that there is no other place where we can find the words of eternal life but Jesus.

> From that time many of his disciples went back, and walked no more with him.
>
> Then said Jesus unto the twelve, Will ye also go away?
>
> Then Simon Peter answered him, Lord, to whom shall we go? Thou hast the words of eternal life.
>
> And we believe and are sure that thou art that Christ, the Son of the living God. (John 6:66–69)

I firmly believe that if anyone truly understands the elemental makeup of what salvation involves, how it is provided by God, how it is appropriated by man, and how it is kept by the power of God, then the only conclusion that is consistent with the whole counsel of God is that salvation is an eternal gift that God gives by a certain specific means: repentance toward God and faith toward our Lord Jesus Christ (Acts 20:21), and that, once the covenant has been entered into, it is irrevocable. The salvation of God is eternal life.

> And this is the record, that God hath given to us eternal life, and this life is in his Son.
>
> He that hath the Son hath life; and he that hath not the Son of God hath not life.
>
> These things have I written unto you that believe on the name of the Son of God; that ye may know that ye have eternal life, and that ye may believe on the name of the Son of God. (1 John 5:11–13)

> Wherefore he is able also to save them to the uttermost that come unto God by him, seeing he ever liveth to make intercession for them. (Hebrews 7:25)

> Now unto him that is able to keep you from falling, and to present you faultless before the presence of his glory with exceeding joy. (Jude 24)

> Blessed be the God and Father of our Lord Jesus Christ, which according to his abundant mercy hath begotten us again unto a lively hope by the resurrection of Jesus Christ from the dead,
>
> To an inheritance incorruptible, and undefiled, and that fadeth not away, reserved in heaven for you,

Who are kept by the power of God through faith unto salvation ready to be revealed in the last time. (1 Peter 1:3–5)

CHAPTER 4

The True Believer Can Never Walk Away

In this chapter, we will examine the biblical paradox of the unbelieving believer. How is it that so many people start out following Jesus and later turn back, usually within a fairly short time? During the time that they follow the Lord, they seem as genuine a believer as anyone else who names the name of Christ. For a season, they look like, walk like, talk like, and act like a child of God.

Then something happens, and they just walk away from the church, the Lord, and the faith itself. Sometimes, they still claim to have faith, but their lives betray the reality of their apostasy of the heart. Do you remember the parable of the wheat and the tares?

> Another parable put he forth unto them, saying, The kingdom of heaven is likened unto a man which sowed good seed in his field:
>
> But while men slept, his enemy came and sowed tares among the wheat, and went his way.
>
> But when the blade was sprung up, and brought forth fruit, then appeared the tares also.
>
> So the servants of the householder came and said unto him, Sir, didst not thou sow good seed in thy field? from whence then hath it tares?

> He said unto them, An enemy hath done
> this. The servants said unto him, Wilt thou then
> that we go and gather them up?
> But he said, Nay; lest while ye gather up the
> tares, ye root up also the wheat with them.
> Let both grow together until the harvest:
> and in the time of harvest I will say to the reap-
> ers, Gather ye together first the tares, and bind
> them in bundles to burn them: but gather the
> wheat into my barn. (Matthew 13:24–30)

In the very beginning, the blade of a wheat plant and the blade of a tare look so much alike that you cannot tell one from the other. However, over time, the wheat plant begins to bear fruit, and the weight of the wheat grain begins to bend the stalk of the wheat down. At the same time, the tare plant continues to grow straight up without any fruit to weigh it down, and eventually, the two plants can be identified, one from the other. That is why the Master told the servants not to try to cut down the tares in the beginning but to let them grow together with the wheat until the harvest because time would tell and reveal which plants were the true wheat and which ones were the tares after all.

Remember, in another place, Jesus admonished, "By their fruits ye shall know them" (Matthew 7:20). When we look upon someone who has made a profession of faith, we often cannot tell the true believer from the unbelieving believer, but over time, they will eventually distinguish themselves, one from the other.

> They went out from us, but they were not
> of us; for if they had been of us, they would no
> doubt have continued with us: but they went out,
> that they might be made manifest that they were
> not all of us. (1 John 2:19)

In this passage, the Lord describes people who assembled with the true believers for a certain period of time but later went out from among them and were thus manifested to have never really been OF those who were members of the true faith. John states that if they had been of us, they would NO DOUBT HAVE CONTINUED WITH US. Their departure from the assembly manifested the fact that they were NEVER TRULY MEMBERS OF THE FAMILY OF GOD.

PEOPLE WONDER, *WHAT ABOUT THE PEOPLE WHO GET SAVED AND LATER WALK AWAY?* THE BIBLE PLAINLY STATES THAT THE TRUE BELIEVER WILL REMAIN AMONG THE FAMILY OF GOD, BUT THAT THOSE WHO WALK AWAY ARE NEVER REALLY NUMBERED AMONG THE TRUE MEMBERS OF THE FAMILY OF GOD.

Now let's go back to our original text in John 6 and take notice of several things that validate the points I have just shared. We zeroed in on only a couple of verses at the top of the chapter, but let's look at the larger context to get some background.

> After these things Jesus went over the sea of Galilee, which is the sea of Tiberias. And a great multitude followed him, because they saw his miracles which he did on them that were dis-eased. (John 6:1–2)

Notice here:

1. Jesus is being followed by a *great multitude.*
2. The reason that the multitude was following Jesus is because "they saw His miracles" of healing those with diseases.

A crowd will gather to see an amazing sideshow where wondrous things are happening, but that doesn't make them true believers and true disciples. They obviously believe that they are witnessing something amazing, and they are mesmerized to a certain extent, but that doesn't make them true believers in the biblical sense, whereby an individual comes into the family of God. They may follow the carnival from place to place to continue to be in the audience to witness the curious phenomena going on under the big tent, but that doesn't make them true disciples.

> Then those men, when they had seen the
> miracle that Jesus did, said, This is of a truth that
> prophet that should come into the world.
> When Jesus therefore perceived that they
> would come and take him by force, to make him
> a king, he departed again into a mountain him-
> self alone. (John 6:14–15)

Clearly, the men that saw His miracles concluded that He was the prophet promised by Moses and the other prophets, and they sought to make Him their king by force, so there is some element of faith involved.

> Jesus answered them and said, Verily, verily,
> I say unto you, Ye seek me, not because ye saw
> the miracles, but because ye did eat of the loaves,
> and were filled.
> Labour not for the meat which perisheth,
> but for that meat which endureth unto everlasting
> life, which the Son of man shall give unto you: for
> him hath God the Father sealed. (John 6:26–27)

Notice here:

1. The reason the multitude was seeking Jesus was because they had seen miracles and had received a free lunch.
2. They were followers (disciples of a sort), but their motive was wrong.
3. They were more interested in material provisions for this life and their earthly bodies than they were in their never-dying souls.

Countless are the numbers of souls, even today, that would seek Jesus and even follow Him to a certain extent, but without the right motive. They love the sideshow elements in many churches and go for the entertainment. They flock to large crusades, where preachers wave their jackets at the audience, and whole sections of the people fall down like a wave. People roll around on the ground making animal noises, or rock concert–loud music pulses out its sensual beat with Jesus's words. But the only thing that is moved is the flesh, as the performers slither and shake their bodies to the raucous music. Many are the "disciples" today who are only interested in following Jesus for what they can get out of Jesus and the church.

Fellowship meal on Sunday with a free meal will always draw a crowd, and if the church were offering free beer and barbecue, the people would line up around the block, but they would fall under the same condemnation as the ones in John 6. In verses 35 through 60, we see the conflict between the Lord and His "disciples" growing into a kind of climax, whereupon the multitude finally reached a critical mass of disagreement with the Lord and made the decision to walk away from Him once and for all.

They had seen the miracles. They had enjoyed the free lunch, but finally, it came down to men still going astray at the heart level, manifesting that rebellion like the tare manifested its own nature over time. Listen to what the Scriptures say.

> Many therefore of his disciples, when they had heard this, said, This is an hard saying; who can hear it?
>
> When Jesus knew in himself that his disciples murmured at it, he said unto them, Doth this offend you?
>
> What and if ye shall see the Son of man ascend up where he was before?
>
> It is the spirit that quickeneth; the flesh profiteth nothing: the words that I speak unto you, they are spirit, and they are life.
>
> But there are some of you that believe not. For Jesus knew from the beginning who they

were that believed not, and who should betray him.

And he said, Therefore said I unto you, that no man can come unto me, except it were given unto him of my Father.

From that time many of his disciples went back, and walked no more with him. (John 6:60–66)

Notice here the following:

1. These were unbelieving disciples or unbelieving believers.
2. Disciples follow their master, and these did for a time (for the wrong reasons and motivation), but when they heard something that they did not want to hear, they walked away and walked no more with him.
3. This proves that they had never fundamentally repented and acknowledged the truth that God's ways and thoughts are higher than man's ways and thoughts.
4. They were STILL GOING THEIR OWN WAY ASTRAY FROM GOD but because it suited their own self-interest to follow Jesus for a time.
5. They did so without ever giving themselves over to Him.
6. They were still the arbiters of every question. They still sat on the throne of their own lives.
7. Jesus KNEW FROM THE BEGINNING WHO THEY WERE THAT BELIEVED NOT, so they were Never Saved. They were never a part of the family of God.

John could say of them truly: "They went out from us, but they were not all of us" (1 John 2:19). IT'S NOT LIKE THESE MEN WERE SAVED AND WALKED AWAY! THEY WERE NEVER SAVED IN THE FIRST PLACE, AND THE SAME IS TRUE OF FOLKS WHO WALK AWAY TODAY! Now consider the stark contrast between the multitude of "disciples" that walked away and Peter.

Then said Jesus unto the twelve, Will ye also go away?

Then Simon Peter answered him, Lord, to whom shall we go? thou hast the words of eternal life.

And we believe and are sure that thou art that Christ, the Son of the living God.

Jesus answered them, Have not I chosen you twelve, and one of you is a devil?

He spake of Judas Iscariot the son of Simon: for he it was that should betray him, being one of the twelve. (John 6:67–71)

1. Notice here that. The genuine believing believer or believing disciple realizes that there is no other place for him or her to go! We believe and are SURE that Jesus Christ is the Son of God and that He ALONE has the words of eternal life, SO WE CANNOT WALK AWAY, EVER!

If you are one of the people who erroneously believe that you can walk away at some point and walk no more with Jesus, YOU MUST REPENT OF THAT BELIEF AND COME TO A KNOWLEDGE OF THE TRUTH! One can walk outside the will of God, but not away from Him. On the other hand, if you don't believe that there would ever be a reason for YOU to walk away from Jesus, but you are concerned about others who might be so inclined because of some verses that seem to indicate that a person can be saved and later lost because they walk away, I want to assure you that all those verses are warnings to dabblers that dip their toes into the water of faith but have never actually taken the plunge with both feet.

Those people ARE NOT SAVED yet and need to be warned, provoked in the proper sense, and exhorted to quit playing around the perimeter of the faith and to finally make their decision to give themselves to Christ before it's eternally too late. Dabblers taste but do not swallow. Dabblers will be damned forever.

CHAPTER 5

Man Is Saved and Kept by the Same Person

Jonah 2:9
Ephesians 2:8–10
1 Peter 1:3–5

Salvation begins with God, proceeds from God to man by the instrument of faith (which is God-given), and is also KEPT by the same means. Jesus is called the "author and finisher" of our faith (Hebrews 12:2). The Bible says that Jesus is "able to save them to the uttermost that comes unto God by Him" (Hebrews 7:25). Jonah said in chapter 2, verse 9, that "salvation is of the Lord" (Jonah 2:9). God is the originator of salvation. It is HIS WORK that provides the redemption and reconciliation for salvation to be possible.

> In whom we have redemption through his blood, the forgiveness of sins, according to the riches of his grace. (Ephesians 1:7)

> And all things are of God, who hath reconciled us to himself by Jesus Christ, and hath given to us the ministry of reconciliation;
> To wit, that God was in Christ, reconciling the world unto himself, not imputing their trespasses unto them; and hath committed unto

us the word of reconciliation. (2 Corinthians 5:18–19)

> For by grace are ye saved through faith; and that not of yourselves: it is the gift of God:
> Not of works, lest any man should boast.
> For we are his workmanship, created in Christ Jesus unto good works, which God hath before ordained that we should walk in them. (Ephesians 2:8–10)

> Blessed be the God and Father of our Lord Jesus Christ, which according to his abundant mercy hath begotten us again unto a lively hope by the resurrection of Jesus Christ from the dead,
> To an inheritance incorruptible, and undefiled, and that fadeth not away, reserved in heaven for you,
> Who are kept by the power of God through faith unto salvation ready to be revealed in the last time. (1 Peter 1:3–5)

Notice here that

1. God does the work to provide the redemption and reconciliation necessary to make the offer of salvation valid,
2. then He works to provide the gift of faith necessary to lay hold of salvation,
3. He begets us unto a lively hope and an inheritance that is incorruptible and undefiled and that fadeth not away.

It is not a mirage of hope that God offers to man, yet when man seeks to cash it in, it turns out to be a pipe dream because God could not secure it as He has promised. It has vanished away.

4. Salvation (biblical salvation) is the result of God's work alone: BOTH in the provision of it and in the maintenance of it as well. God saves, and God keeps through the provision of the faith, of which He is the author and finisher.

CHAPTER 6

The Descriptive Terms God Uses Teach Eternal Security

John 10:28
John 3:16 and 1 John 5:11–13

One of the reasons I am personally so convinced that English-speaking Christians should use only the King James Bible is because of the method of biblical translation used in modern translations, called dynamic equivalence. For those of you who have never done research into the question of what the basic differences are between the various English translations, I will make it very simple, because it is not really a part of what I am writing this to explain. Dynamic equivalence is a method of Bible translation that seeks to communicate the main idea of a particular passage of the Scripture instead of the actual best word-for-word translation. This is the method used in ALL of the popular modern translations.

HerI is the problem with that approach. It robs us of the exact words that God spoke by the Holy Spirit, and specific words have specific and definite meanings. When the translators seek to give the meaning of the passage, they are taking upon themselves the role of interpreter, and the result is more of a paraphrase than an actual word-for-word translation. The paraphrase is filtered through the interpretive paradigm of the translator, and that can lead to false conclusions about the teachings of the Bible. That is why it is vital to start with the exact words, at least as closely as can be found, for a word-for-word translation from the original Greek and Hebrew into whatever language One might translate into. Having said all of that, it is important to look at the exact words used in the King James Bible that were translated with formal equivalence, the method whereby an exact word-for-word translation is sought, leaving the interpretation to the reader in accordance with the illumination of the Holy Spirit.

> And I give unto them eternal life; and they
> shall never perish, neither shall any man pluck
> them out of my hand. (John 10:28)

If Jesus meant what He said and said what He meant, then the word eternal is significant because the word means forever. If the gift that Jesus gives is eternal, then it will have no end. Thus it cannot be received and later lost. The descriptive term here has a definite, specific meaning that is not in doubt.

> For God so loved the world, that he gave his
> only begotten Son, that whosoever believeth in
> him should not perish, but have everlasting life.
> (John 3:16)

Now just as was true of the passage in John 10:28, we have no reason to doubt that Jesus meant what He said and said what He meant, so we start by asking, "What did he actually say?"

What was the term that He used to describe the promise of God toward the believing sinner in response to the Good News of the Gospel? Jesus said that the Father's intention was that whoever believes in His Son would have everlasting life. Now just as eternal life must mean forever life because eternity will last forever, the same is true with everlasting life. In fact, everlasting is a perfect synonym for the word eternal because they both mean the exact same thing. One might ask, "How long do eternal life and everlasting life last?"

My own hunch is that you do not have to bring in a rocket scientist to figure that out.

> And this is the record, that God hath given to us eternal life, and this life is in his Son.
> He that hath the Son hath life; and he that hath not the Son of God hath not life.
> These things have I written unto you that believe on the name of the Son of God; that ye may know that ye have eternal life, and that ye may believe on the name of the Son of God. (1 John 5:11–13)

One of the saddest things I can think of would be to ignore the record that God has given to all of us for the purpose of letting us KNOW whether or not we have eternal life while we are still alive in this world. Most likely the greatest fear that any man has is the fear of death and the anxiety over where he will spend eternity. If God has directly addressed this fear and anxiety, it would be just like the devil to rob man of that assurance by casting doubt on these verses. But they should be very clear in their meaning to every student of the Bible because of the descriptive term used two times: eternal life. Again God tells us that He has given us a record of His having given eternal life in the person of His Son and that if we truly have the Son, we do truly have eternal life.

If eternal means forever, which it plainly does, then these verses should set aside our fears and anxiety about death once and for all because if we actually possess it, by the very definition of the term eternal, it can never be taken away or rescinded.

CHAPTER 7

The Definitive Words and Phrases That Accompany the Descriptive Terms Teach Eternal Security

John 10:28
John 3:16–17 and John 5:24

The context defines the terms by comparison.

1. I give unto them eternal life, and they shall never perish.

Notice here that the descriptive term used to describe the GIFT of God is eternal life, and then the definitive words or phrases that accompany eternal life explain that the recipients of eternal life shall never perish. Thus, one of the definitions of eternal life is that its possessors will never perish, which is a reference to the second death (John 10:28).

Revelation 20:14–15 tells us that the second death is to be cast into the lake of fire, the place of eternal separation from God.

2. Neither shall any man pluck them out of My hand.

Here we see eternal life as being defined as being securely in the hand of Jesus Christ. Our security is dependent upon the strength of the hand of the One who holds us.

If Jesus is GOD, and He clearly claims to be, then we cannot be removed from the omnipotent hand that secures us. Now someone might say, "Yes, but what if a believer turns away from Jesus and no longer wants to be secured thusly in His hand?" My answer to that question is twofold: First, read again about repentance and the attitudinal aspect of salvation. IF one is genuinely saved, that individual would never have any interest in being removed from the hand of God. Secondly, the verse says, "Neither shall ANY MAN pluck them out." You are a man, so YOU ARE INCLUDED in that inability to pluck yourself out of His hand (John 10:28)!

3. No man is ABLE to pluck them out of My Father's hand.

This is just the same statement as above, but with GREATER EMPHASIS because Jesus is now appealing to the believer's faith in the strength of the FATHER's hand to convey the confidence that His sheep can have in the eternal security of their own soul.

4. Should not perish but have everlasting life.
5. In John 3:16, the Lord reverses the order, placing the definitive phrase before the descriptive words. Here, the descriptive term is everlasting life, and the term is defined as meaning that its possessor should not perish. This also proves that eternal life from John 10:28 and everlasting life from this verse are synonymous because they are linked to the exact same definition.
6. That the world through Him might be saved.

This definitive phrase links back to the descriptive term of everlasting life in the previous verse. By that comparison, it also serves to define the term saved as being synonymous with possessing everlasting life.

7. Hath everlasting life and shall not come into condemnation.

This definitive phrase is clearly an affirmation that once a soul has been saved and passed from a status of being under condemnation to a status of no longer being under condemnation, he or she will not be able to come back under condemnation—meaning to be lost, in an unsaved condition, headed for hell and the lake of fire—again afterward.

> He that believeth on him is not condemned:
> but he that believeth not is condemned already,
> because he hath not believed in the name of the
> only begotten Son of God. (John 3:18)

Prior to faith in Christ and the salvation that is secured thereby (John 3:16–17), a man is "condemned already." Once a man has been genuinely saved, he is moved to a place of being not condemned (John 3:18). Once he has entered that place of being not condemned, Jesus says that he will not come back into condemnation again in the future.

8. BUT IS PASSED FROM DEATH TO LIFE.

Note the contrasting conjunction but. A contrasting conjunction is a word that ties two statements together that are different from each other OR the opposite of each other.

We might say, "Sally had a blue dress, but Mary wore a pink one to the show," or we could say: "Billy likes going UP on the elevator, but Johnny likes to go DOWN." Here, in John 5:24, the Lord contrasts coming under condemnation with passing from death to life. Passing from death unto life is tied with having everlasting life. So clearly, once an individual has been saved and has everlasting life, he got there by passing from death unto life, and he cannot come into condemnation again in the future. These are just a small fraction of the number of verses that could be cited that state clearly and categorically that salvation is eternally secure.

CHAPTER 8

The Tense of the Verbs Used to Describe the Time Frame of the Gift of Eternal Life Teach Eternal Security

John 10:28
John 3:16
John 5:24
1 John 5:11–13

1. I GIVE (present tense) unto them eternal life.

    Notice the gift of eternal life is given in the present tense, not at some point in the future. Salvation is an instantaneous event, NOT A PROCESS, and it is NOT held back until a certain future point, when man has died and is already incapable of sinning in a grievous enough manner to warrant taking back the gift or when he is past a point in time when he can turn and walk away from the Lord. Neither is salvation given in time instantaneously at a certain point in someone's life with the disclaimer that it can be forfeited later if the recipient does not do a certain thing or group of things. That would make salvation based upon works! If not in the obtaining of it, then at least in the maintaining of it, AND THAT IS JUST NOT BIBLICAL!

2. Should not perish but HAVE (present tense) everlasting life.

3. HATH (present tense) everlasting life.
4. Is (present tense) passed from death unto life.
5. He that HATH (present tense) the SON HATH (present tense) life.
6. That ye may know that YE HAVE (present tense) eternal life.

Since the gift of eternal life or everlasting life is given by God to the believer IN THE PRESENT TENSE (while the sinner is still alive and at the time that he believes in a scripturally saving manner) and since eternal life and everlasting LIFE WILL LAST FOREVER, the Bible clearly teaches the doctrine of eternal security for the genuine biblical believer. Now obviously, much more could be said to expand the length of this study itself, but I will leave this topic with the reader by stating that, in my opinion, enough has already been said to establish the point being made herein.

CHAPTER 9

Two Rules of Hermeneutics That Support the Teaching of Eternal Security

For those of you who may have never heard of the word *hermeneutics*, let me assure you that you are not alone. It is not a word that is generally part of anyone's conversation except for Theologians (people who study to know about God). The word *hermeneutics* refers to the study of the science of interpreting the message of the Scriptures. To make it simple to understand, there are Rules that have been discovered from the study of the Bible that enable the student of the Scriptures to be able to interpret Its message correctly.

Those rules apply to every individual who would seek to understand the Bible, and to ignore or deliberately break those rules will inevitably lead to a misunderstanding of the Bible's message.

1. The Bible does not contain any genuine contradictions within its pages.
2. You must never begin to build any doctrine upon an obscure text, which clearly contradicts the statements within a clear text, where the meaning cannot be in dispute.

Okay, let me start this portion with a brief explanation of the word *obscure* for anyone who might need that to be given. The word *obscure* has the idea of being unclear, like looking through a fog. The idea is that enough of what you are looking at has been slightly hidden, so what you are visualizing can be easily misinterpreted. Imagine you are driving down a country road that is unfamiliar to you, and you are dealing with a thick fog. Something runs across the road up ahead in a flash. You see a shape, but between the darkness and the thick fog reflecting your headlights back into your eyes, you cannot be sure if it is a large, skinny dog or a small deer with absolute certainty.

Now imagine that same event on a clear day in broad daylight. You are fully alert and paying attention to the road and your surroundings. You are not being distracted by the radio or someone else in the car. You had a good night's sleep, and you are not daydreaming.

The animal crosses the road, and your vision is clear. Your mind is not trying to process a hundred other things, and you see crystal clear what has just occurred. Your mind instantly recognizes what you are looking at and can correctly process what has just occurred. It was clearly a dog, not a deer or anything else, for that matter.

Many times people study the Bible, and they read something that has a meaning that is crystal Clear. Other times they read verses that COULD be a DOG OR a DEER, but the verse itself just CANNOT be USED as the BASIS for a DOGMATIC conclusion.

When you have a verse that IS CRYSTAL CLEAR as it relates to stating a particular doctrine or teaching, and you find another verse that is not so clear that COULD be stating something that is CONTRARY to what is stated clearly in the other passage, those two rules of hermeneutics must be applied to your study. First, the cloudy verse cannot be stating something that is a genuine contradiction to that which is stated in the clear verse. Secondly, you cannot exclude the clear verse FIRST and START to BUILD your doctrine upon your interpretation of the verse that is not clear if that conclusion would clearly contradict the teaching derived from the clear verse. Let me give you an example that will probably ruffle some tail feathers of what I am talking about.

The Pentecostal Church and Charismatic churches make a big deal out of the supernatural gift of speaking in tongues. They make loud claims about the importance of speaking in tongues and exhort ALL of their people to seek this spiritual gift. Some even believe that a person must be able to speak in tongues as evidence that the person is genuinely saved. Consider the following FACTS.

1. NOWHERE does the Bible clearly state or even imply that there are TWO DISTINCTLY DIFFERENT GIFTS of speaking in tongues. NOWHERE!

2. In Acts 2, where the Pentecostals get their denominational name from and where speaking in tongues is FIRST MENTIONED, the gift CLEARLY and UNQUESTIONABLY refers to KNOWN HUMAN LANGUAGES, which are unknown to the speakers but are known by the listeners and actually LISTED in Acts 2:1–11. THIS IS NOT EVEN DEBATABLE!

3. ALL Pentecostal and Charismatic missionaries to other countries GO TO LANGUAGE SCHOOL before they begin their ministries to other language-speaking people. NONE OF THEM JUST GO TO JAPAN AND BEGIN SPEAKING JAPANESE!

4. Clearly, the Pentecostals and Charismatics today ARE NOT EXERCISING THE SAME GIFT OF TONGUES AS THE FIRST CHURCH AT JERUSALEM DID ON THE DAY OF PENTECOST.

5. The Pentecostals deliberately ignore the clear teaching from Acts 2:1–11 regarding the practice of biblical tongues and have chosen to build their doctrine of speaking in tongues based on obscure passages.

1 Corinthians chapters 12–14 are actually written to correct a carnal church that was trying to vaunt their spirituality by the practice of counterfeit gifts of the Spirit.

Instead of acknowledging the corrective nature of the entire book of 1 Corinthians to a group of carnal baby Christians, the Pentecostals and Charismatics use those chapters as the basis to justify the exercise of something clearly contrary to the clearly defined gift of the Holy Spirit that was bestowed upon the first church to communicate the Gospel to multitudes of visitors to Jerusalem from other language groups on the Day of Pentecost in the first century.

6. For the Pentecostals and the Charismatics to be correct about their views on the spiritual gift of speaking in tongues, THERE HAS TO BE EITHER TWO DIFFERENT GIFTS OR TYPES OF THE GIFT OF TONGUES BECAUSE THEY CERTAINLY ARE NOT EXERCISING THE SAME GIFT AS IS DEFINED in Acts 2:1–11.

7. Since God claims to NOT BE THE AUTHOR OF CONFUSION (1 Corinthians 14:33), and since there are clearly two different things in operation between the Acts 2 tongues and what is being practiced among Pentecostals and Charismatics today, either I should not be in confusion, or God should have made it clear that there are TWO LEGITIMATE GIFTS by the same name, or the Pentecostals and Charismatics HAVE ERRED in the way they have handled the Word of God, and they should CEASE THEIR UNBIBLICAL PRACTICE.

8. No one can argue the FACT that TODAY there is MUCH CONFUSION among believers about the subject of the spiritual gift of speaking in tongues. If the Pentecostal and Charismatic practice were legitimate, all God would have had to do to clear up the confusion would be to state clearly that there were two legitimate exercises of that gift: one being the specific human languages and the other being completely unintelligible utterances. We KNOW that the human languages that were known by the listeners but unknown by the speakers were a definite legitimate exercise of the spiritual gift of speaking in tongues because God made that absolutely clear in Acts 2:1–11.

However, God said that the Corinthians were ignorant of spiritual gifts and that He did not want them to remain so (1 Corinthians 12:1). We know the Corinthians were carnal and that He had to speak to them as babies and not as spiritually mature (1 Corinthians 3:1–4).

We know that the purpose for which God had given spiritual gifts was for the benefit or edification of every man (1 Corinthians 12:7). We know that the Corinthians were speaking in unknown and unintelligible utterances in order to edify themselves individually (1 Corinthians 14:1–4), even though no one else benefited. There is so much more that could be said.

Now I am not here trying to bash on the Pentecostals or the Charismatics per se. What I am seeking to do is to show, by that illustration, how the clear teaching from clear verses should not be ignored, and official teachings should not be built on unclear verses that contradict the clear teaching from the clear verses.

What the aforementioned groups have done is to build a whole body of teaching that affirms the exact opposite of what the BIBLE affirms and actually denies what the Bible actually does teach. In relation to the doctrine of salvation and whether or not the soul of a truly saved man or woman is eternally secure, we must be careful to look for all the verses we can that deal with the subject and lay them out in order. The first verses in the order of importance, as it relates to discovering how to rightly divide the word of truth on that (or frankly, any) doctrine, will be the ones that make the clearest statements on the subject. After the clearest verses, those less and less clear will follow in their order, from the most clear to the least clear. After those are assembled, we will be able to begin to get a handle on what "the whole counsel of God" teaches, and we will be able to distinguish what is a little left of center and what is a little right of center in the straight and narrow path of life.

CHAPTER 10

Some Summary Statements Based upon Some Clear Scriptures

John 10:27–30 and 2 Timothy 2:15

1. The ultimate question is NOT, "Can you be legitimately saved by grace through faith and then somehow SO SIN or SO WALK AWAY FROM THE FAITH as to be ultimately eternally lost?"
2. The ultimate question is, "WHAT KIND OF FAITH IS IT that actually secures eternal life for those who possess it?"

> For by grace are ye SAVED THROUGH FAITH;
> and that not of yourselves: it is the gift of God:
> Not of works, lest any man should boast.
> For we are his workmanship, created in Christ Jesus unto good works, which God hath before ordained that we should walk in them. (Ephesians 2:8–10)

> For God so loved the world, that he gave his only begotten Son, that whosoever believeth in him should not perish, but have everlasting life.

> For God sent not his Son into the world to condemn the world; but that the world through him might be saved.
>
> He that believeth on him is not condemned: but he that believeth not is condemned already, because he hath not believed in the name of the only begotten Son of God. (John 3:16–18)

> Verily, verily, I say unto you, He that heareth my word, and believeth on him that sent me, hath everlasting life, and shall not come into condemnation; but is passed from death unto life. (John 5:24)

> My sheep hear my voice, and I know them, and they follow me:
>
> And I give unto them eternal life; and they shall never perish, neither shall any man pluck them out of my hand. (John 10:27)

LESSONS CLEARLY TAUGHT IN THESE VERSES:

a. FAITH is the KEY to receiving salvation from God; saving faith is a GIFT from God.

b. Salvation is not the PRODUCT of man's works or worthiness; it is by the GRACE AND WORKS of God.

c. One of the characteristics of salvation is eternal or everlasting life.

d. The giving and possessing of eternal life is something that is done in the PRESENT TENSE.

e. Those described as being saved and possessing eternal life are affirmed to be EXEMPT from COMING INTO (something in the future from the present point in time) CONDEMNATION.

f. The Lord's TRUE sheep hear His voice and FOLLOW Him.

g. There is nothing that ANY MAN can DO to REMOVE one of the Lord's own sheep from His hand.

> Blessed be the God and Father of our Lord Jesus Christ, which according to his abundant mercy hath begotten us again unto a lively hope by the resurrection of Jesus Christ from the dead,
>
> To an inheritance incorruptible, and undefiled, and that fadeth not away, reserved in heaven for you,
>
> Who are kept by the power of God through faith unto salvation ready to be revealed in the last time. (1 Peter 1:3–5)

> Not by works of righteousness which we have done, but according to his mercy he saved us, by the washing of regeneration, and renewing of the Holy Ghost;
>
> Which he shed on us abundantly through Jesus Christ our Saviour;
>
> That being justified by his grace, we should be made heirs according to the hope of eternal life.
>
> This is a faithful saying, and these things I will that thou affirm constantly, that they which have believed in God might be careful to maintain good works. These things are good and profitable unto men. (Titus 3:5–8)

LESSONS CLEARLY TAUGHT IN THESE VERSES:

a. The new birth that occurs at salvation is the product of God's abundant mercy and grace and not on the basis of man's good deeds or works of righteousness. Mercy is the withholding of punishment that is deserved. Forty-two times in the Old Testament, God tells His people that His mercy endures forever. Each of the twenty-six verses in Psalm 136 ends with the phrase: "For His mercy endureth forever." Mercy withdrawn does not endure.

b. Man's justification in the sight of God is based on God's grace. In other words, it is based on a blessing from God that man DOES NOT DESERVE.

c. The born-again child of God is given an inheritance, which is RESERVED in heaven for him or her.

d. The person who is born again is KEPT BY GOD'S POWER unto salvation.

e. The God-given faith that produced salvation (Ephesians 2) also serves to KEEP one saved by God's power (1 Peter 1:5).

f. God affirms that those who "HAVE BELIEVED IN GOD" should "BE CAREFUL TO MAINTAIN GOOD WORKS." Thus, good works should indeed follow saving faith, but THEY DO NOT PRODUCE OR KEEP SALVATION. This also agrees with Ephesians 2:8–10, which states that salvation is the product of God's workmanship and that salvation is UNTO GOOD WORKS but is not produced by man's good works. It is important to see that good works are THE FRUIT OF SALVATION, NOT THE ROOT OF SALVATION. SAVING FAITH IS THE GIFT OF GOD THAT SAVES AND KEEPS. If we understand those things, WE CAN BETTER UNDERSTAND WHY SALVATION IS ETERNALLY SECURE.

Truly, as Jonah said in chapter 2:9: "SALVATION IS OF THE LORD."

CHAPTER 11

What about the Verses That Seem to Teach That a Person Can Be Saved and Later Lose His Salvation?

Even though there are so many verses that clearly teach that salvation is eternally secure, there are some verses in the Bible that SEEM, to some folks, to teach that saving faith can be embraced for a period of time in an individual's life and then later renounced or repudiated in such a way as to exclude that one from the blessed status of being one of the saved who are bound for heaven upon their exit from this physical life on Earth.

There are also some folks that believe that an individual can be genuinely saved at a certain point in time but later sin in such a grievous manner as to LOSE that salvation and thus need to be saved again or be subject to suffering the torments of the damned forever.

I will readily agree that if one does not CORRECTLY DEFINE THE FAITH THAT SAVES, there are several verses that become confusing and seem to imply that salvation cannot be eternally secure, at least until after one's death, whereupon the capacity to choose to walk away from the faith and the potential to sin in such a grievous manner as described above is presumably no longer a potential reality.

HOWEVER, my firm conviction is that the problem is resolved when ONE CORRECTLY DEFINES JUST EXACTLY WHAT QUALIFIES AS "SAVING FAITH." I would like to begin our examination of saving faith by first looking at a passage of Scripture that many folks think teaches that salvation is the product of FAITH PLUS WORKS. Because they believe that, they are then forced to conclude that salvation is at least partly based upon our performance. That is not what is actually being taught in the passage.

What it IS TEACHING is that there are different KINDS of FAITH and that professing believers needs to realize that men need more than our lip service testifying to them that we are believers. Men need to see the EVIDENCE OF our faith for them to see our testimony as justified in their sight. That passage is James 2:14–26.

I. James clearly teaches that there are at least THREE TYPES OF FAITH in the eyes of God.

> Demonic Faith, Dead Faith, and Working Faith, which IS SAVING FAITH.
> Thou believest that there is one God; thou doest well: the devils also believe, and tremble.
> But wilt thou know, O vain man, that faith without works is dead? (James 2:19–20)

Consider first WHO JAMES IS. James is the half-brother of the Lord Jesus. He became the primary leader of the first church in Jerusalem. He was certainly someone who would be IN THE KNOW as far as the question of SAVING FAITH.

A. There IS A DEMONIC FAITH! James states that DEMONS BELIEVE AND TREMBLE because of their faith.

There are many things that could be said here, but it should be clear to any honest person that God is making a distinction regarding the quality of faith in these verses. Thus He distinguishes between one kind of faith and another. Notice that He DOES NOT SAY that the DEMONS DO NOT BELIEVE, but that THEIR FAITH MOVES THEM TO FEARFULNESS. It does not change their BEHAVIOR. It does not lead them to REPENTANCE: just "a certain fearful looking for of judgment and fiery indignation, which SHALL DEVOUR THE ADVERSARIES" of God one day, as God refers to in the book of Hebrews chapter 10 (Hebrews 10:27). This fearfulness is seen in the New Testament in different places (see Matthew 8:28–29, Mark 5:2–7, and Luke 8:26–28).

> And when he was come to the other side into the country of the Gergesenes, there met him two possessed with devils, coming out of the tombs, exceeding fierce, so that no man might pass by that way.
> And, behold, they cried out, saying, What have we to do with thee, Jesus, thou Son of God? art thou come hither to torment us before the time? (Matthew 8:28–29)

Clearly, the demons were genuinely in fear because they BELIEVED in God and that HE had appointed a DAY OF JUDGMENT, which would result in their being TORMENTED. WE MUST ASK OURSELVES: "WHAT KIND OF FAITH DO I POSSESS?"

If the Bible clearly teaches that salvation is by grace through FAITH, and the demons of HELL BELIEVE and are so moved with fear that they actually tremble at the thought of the torment that awaits them, then why will they not be saved unless it is a DIFFERENT QUALITY OF FAITH that God is looking for to bring a soul into a place where he or she will not be condemned? How SAD it is that many folks who profess to believe in Jesus Christ do not even possess as much faith as the demons of hell.

The demons of hell are MOVED with FEAR enough to tremble because of their faith, yet many professing believers are not moved at all to do anything because of their faith. These are the FALSE PROFESSORS who possess a DEAD FAITH that James refers to in chapter 2, verse 14 (James 2:14).

> What doth it profit, my brethren, though a man say he hath faith, and have not works? can faith save him? (James 2:14)

> Even so faith, if it hath not works, is dead,
> being alone. (James 2:17)

B.   There IS a DEAD FAITH.

Dead faith may be ardently proclaimed to be real, but it is never proven to be REAL BY ACTIONS. James 2:14–26 is one of the sections of Scripture that contains statements that are very often taken out of context and misunderstood to teach that salvation is based upon doing good works. However, that is not the emphasis of this section of Scripture. Rather, the emphasis is on presenting the reality that there are different kinds of faith THAT PRODUCE DIFFERENT KINDS OF RESULTS.

This will be a slight digression, but to understand what James is saying about "faith without works is dead" and "can faith save him" is not to be viewed as an equation for salvation. He is not saying that faith PLUS works equals salvation. It is not like one plus one equals two. That is where the problem of misinterpretation lies! He is not saying that faith plus works save; he is saying that true saving faith PRODUCES WORKS. The works are the outgrowth of saving faith. Real, true faith will produce fruit. Even the demons' faith produces an appropriate action: fear. The kind of faith that James characterizes as DEAD faith doesn't produce ANYTHING. It is merely a FALSE PROFESSION!

A MAN CAN SAY he has faith without doing anything that proves the legitimacy of his claim, but he can't PROVE his faith WITHOUT ACTION. THAT is what James is saying! In fact, he is asserting that the LACK of ACTION PROVES the illegitimacy of the claim. He says, for example, take Rahab and Abraham's faith and how they demonstrated the reality of it BY THEIR ACTIONS. He says you can say you have faith all day long, but you can't SHOW your faith WITHOUT ACTION.

> Yea, a man may say, Thou hast faith, and I
> have works: shew me thy faith without thy works,

and I will shew thee my faith by my works.
(James 2:18)

He is telling his audience: "Okay, you can SAY you have faith, but what if someone challenges your profession? You can't prove that your faith is legitimate WITHOUT ACTION." The fellow challenges you to PROVE that you are a believer. He says that he will be able to prove his faith by his actions accordingly, but that the guy can't prove he is a believer by just SAYING he is one. James goes on to argue that that kind of profession of faith is illegitimate in the exact same way as the profession about concern for the welfare of an individual who is starving and freezing to death is illegitimate when you say, "Be ye warmed and filled," but you do nothing to actually aid them in their freezing and starving state.

You don't really care that they are freezing and starving if you don't DO SOMETHING ABOUT IT!

Jesus said in John 14:15: "If ye love Me, KEEP MY COMMANDMENTS" (John 14:15). He said in Luke 6:46: "And why call ye Me, Lord, Lord, and do not the things which I say?" (Luke 6:46). That brings us to our third kind of faith, which James is referring to in the Scriptures listed above, and we need to be aware of this type of faith in order to understand why saving faith works and why saving faith will produce eternal security for everyone who possessed it.

C.   There IS a SAVING FAITH THAT WORKS.

It is NOT FAITH PLUS WORKS that equals salvation, but faith that works.

You may THINK that is a distinction without a difference, but there is a great difference because the belief that it is faith plus works requires faith to be placed in something that MAN DOES. a Belief that salvation is produced by a faith THAT works PUTS SALVATION BEFORE THE ACTION and understands that the action GROWS OUT of the teaching that is believed. The teaching that is believed is that MAN COULD NOT DO ANYTHING TO OBTAIN GOD'S FORGIVENESS. Man's righteousness is like a filthy rag in the eyes of God (Isaiah

64:6), so it cannot reconcile anyone. That is WHY it is "NOT by works of righteousness which we have done, but according to His mercy He saved us" (Titus 3:5).

Jesus alone "knew no sin."

Jesus alone "did no sin."

Jesus alone "washed us from our sins in His own blood" (Revelation 1:5).

Jesus alone "bare our sins in His own body on the tree" (1 Peter 2:24).

Jesus alone was "made to be sin for us, that we might be made the righteousness of God in Him" (2 Corinthians 5:21).

Jesus alone "died for our sins according to the Scriptures, was buried, and rose again the third day according to the Scriptures" (1 Corinthians 15:3–4).

The faith that saves believes that Jesus alone was able to fully satisfy the righteous demands of the law, pay the fearful penalty for man's failure to do so, and then rise victorious over death, the grave, and the one who had the power of death, the devil. There is not a single thing that man can do to enter into that work. It is the work of GOD ALONE IN CHRIST, RECONCILING THE WORLD TO HIMSELF. Saving faith hears the word of truth, the gospel of Jesus Christ as our ONLY HOPE of heaven, and reaches out to God BY FAITH to take hold of that lively hope of eternal life through Jesus Christ and HIS WORK ALONE.

To believe that salvation is obtained in any other way is to believe another gospel—one which is not taught in the Holy Scriptures. Now BECAUSE God loved us so much that He did all of the work to provide salvation, and because our hearts have received that message, WE LOVE HIM BECAUSE HE FIRST LOVED US, and that love because of that faith MOTIVATES OUR GOOD WORKS. Therefore, the good works that any true believer in the TRUE GOSPEL performs ARE THE FRUIT OF THAT FAITH, NOT SOMETHING IN ADDITION TO THAT FAITH, which coupled together with that faith produces salvation. Being saved or not being saved had NOTHING TO DO WITH SOMETHING THAT ORIG-INATES WITH THE ACTIONS OF ANY UNSAVED MAN. Salvation is based upon having the right beliefs.

Consider the scriptures:

> For in Jesus Christ neither circumcision availeth any thing, nor uncircumcision; but faith which worketh by love. (Galatians 5:6)

The only thing that AVAILS with God has nothing to do with the LAW or any kind of works of righteousness. Circumcision represented the keeping of the Old Testament Law. Uncircumcision represented the failure to keep the Law. Paul is saying that salvation is not about our actions. Salvation is all about our faith—what we believe.

The KIND OF FAITH that AVAILS with God is a faith that works BY LOVE. That is a descriptive statement, not a formula of faith plus works equaling salvation. It describes a KIND of faith—it is a faith THAT works. Is the motivation for the WORKS A HOPE or a FAITH in the WORKS as being a basis for EARNING favor with God and His salvation? Or is the motivation for the WORKS the LOVE that is in the heart of the believer because of the incredible magnitude of the love of God toward us? It is the believer's faith in the love of God toward us that motivates our work FOR HIM. HIS WORK IN PROVIDING US with salvation that we were TOTALLY INCAPABLE of providing for ourselves PROVES His love for us, creates a RECIPROCAL love for Him, and MOTIVATES OUR WORKS FOR HIM.

> For God so loved the world, that he gave his only begotten Son, that whosoever believeth in him should not perish, but have everlasting life. (John 3:16)

> But God commendeth his love toward us, in that, while we were yet sinners, Christ died for us. (Romans 5:8)

> We love him, because he first loved us. (1 John 4:19)

We are made aware of God's love toward us through the Gospel of Jesus and because of that love toward us, we are MOVED TO LOVE GOD BACK, and THAT LOVE MOTIVATES OUR WORKS. Thus, faith works BY love. That is the KIND of faith that saves a soul. The works do not produce salvation in any way. It is the love, because of the faith in God's love for us, that actually motivates our labors of love toward Him.

Since good works have nothing to do with producing salvation, bad works (or sinful works) have no power to retract salvation. We are saved by the power of God, AND we are also kept by the power of God through faith unto salvation. The faith that saves is the GIFT of God. Truly, salvation IS OF THE LORD! That is why it is irrevocable. That is why NO MAN can pluck the child of God out of His hands. To really understand why salvation is eternally secure, one needs to truly understand the basis upon which the Lord GIVES it in the first place. Once that is nailed down, the confusing verses don't cause that many problems anymore.

Getting back to James 2:14–26:

Some people get very confused when they read some of the things James wrote there unless they understand the context of James's argument.

He is stating that there are two judges when it comes to a man's faith: one is God, and the other is fellow men. God knows the hearts of all men. God doesn't really need a demonstration to PROVE the legitimacy of a man's faith the way that a man does. A man needs to SEE the PROOF of man's faith in his works to see him as being justified before God.

James says, in essence, that you can say you believe all day long, but a man will need to see the proof in your actions. Otherwise, he will conclude that yours is a false profession, like the guy expressing concern for another who says, "Be ye warmed and filled," but doesn't do anything to help. God knew that Abraham believed Him long before Abraham's faith was demonstrated by His offering up Isaac, and that is why Abraham was saved by faith long before Isaac was even born. Men, who cannot see and know the human heart as God does, need to see the evidence by our actions. That is why James says that a man might challenge the professing believer and say, "Shew me thy faith without thy works, and I will shew thee my faith BY MY WORKS."

He also gives the example of Rahab and her hiding of the spies for the same reason: to establish that a man can look at the actions of another person and see the reality of that person's genuine faith. In that sense, a man is justified in the eyes of another man by his works because the works demonstrate the reality of his faith. Just like the sacrifice of Jesus "commendeth [or demonstrated] His love toward us" (Romans 5:8).

We know the reality of God's declaration of love toward us because of His demonstration. God knows the reality of our faith in Him without any deeds having to be performed to prove its reality. However, if our faith is legitimate saving faith, it will work, and man will be able to look upon our actions and know what God knows without having to see the demonstration. James is making the point that men need to be able to see their faith IN THEIR ACTIONS because that is the only way they will know it is legitimate. An expression of concern for another without any action that verifies the concern expressed is just offering lip service.

It is (to use James' expression) a "DEAD" CONCERN. There is no life to it, no reality to it. The same is true of an expression of faith that has no action to verify its reality. It is DEAD FAITH!

That is why he says, "Faith without works is dead, being alone." The FACT that man is justified in the sight of God apart from ANY WORKS OF RIGHTEOUSNESS may be clearly seen in the verses immediately below.

> Now we know that what things soever the law saith, it saith to them who are under the law: that every mouth may be stopped, and all the world may become guilty before God.
>
> Therefore by the deeds of the law there shall no flesh be justified in his sight: for by the law is the knowledge of sin.
>
> But now the righteousness of God without the law is manifested, being witnessed by the law and the prophets;

Even the righteousness of God which is by faith of Jesus Christ unto all and upon all them that believe: for there is no difference:

For all have sinned, and come short of the glory of God;

Being justified freely by his grace through the redemption that is in Christ Jesus:

Whom God hath set forth to be a propitiation through faith in his blood, to declare his righteousness for the remission of sins that are past, through the forbearance of God;

To declare, I say, at this time his righteousness: that he might be just, and the justifier of him which believeth in Jesus.

Where is boasting then? It is excluded. By what law? of works? Nay: but by the law of faith.

Therefore we conclude that a man is justified by faith without the deeds of the law. (Romans 3:19–28)

So often a careful reading of the overall context will clear up the confusing verses just like in James. A classic passage that confuses folks and leads some to doubt eternal security is Hebrews 6:1–6.

Therefore leaving the principles of the doctrine of Christ, let us go on unto perfection; not laying again the foundation of repentance from dead works, and of faith toward God,

Of the doctrine of baptisms, and of laying on of hands, and of resurrection of the dead, and of eternal judgment.

And this will we do, if God permit.

For it is impossible for those who were once enlightened, and have tasted of the heavenly gift, and were made partakers of the Holy Ghost,

> And have tasted the good word of God, and
> the powers of the world to come,
> If they shall fall away, to renew them again
> unto repentance; seeing they crucify to them-
> selves the Son of God afresh, and put him to an
> open shame. (Hebrews 6:1–6)

This section is one of the greatest stumbling blocks for people when it comes to seeing salvation as being eternally secure. They also couple the words "if they shall FALL AWAY" with a portion of the verse in Galatians 5:4, which says, "YE ARE FALLEN FROM GRACE," and they conclude that an individual can, in fact, be saved in a state of grace and later FALL AWAY from it and thus LOSE his or her salvation. However, that is NOT what is being taught in either passage.

To understand why that is a misinterpretation of the passage, the student of Scripture must take a look at the larger context, which includes a portion of chapter 5 as well as additional verses in chapter 6. After reading the larger context, one comes to the realization that the author (I personally believe that the human author is Paul), under the inspiration of the Holy Spirit, is referring in verses 1–6 to what I have dubbed as DABBLERS and not those who are truly committed to the Lord Jesus Christ and the faith that bears His name.

The passage serves as a great warning to those who are curious about the faith but not committed to it, who have experimented with the idea of saving faith but have not truly experienced it. Those spoken about are not falling away from the faith but from the appearance of faith. They are pretenders like Judas, who was not a TRUE BELIEVER from the very beginning (John 6:64).

Judas certainly had the appearance of being a follower and a true disciple of Jesus, but HE NEVER WAS. CONSIDER THE LARGER CONTEXT: Hebrews 5:11–6:15.

> For the earth which drinketh in the rain
> that cometh oft upon it, and bringeth forth herbs
> meet for them by whom it is dressed, receiveth
> blessing from God:

> But that which beareth thorns and briers is rejected, and is nigh unto cursing; whose end is to be burned.
>
> But, beloved, we are persuaded better things of you, and things that accompany salvation, though we thus speak.
>
> For God is not unrighteous to forget your work and labour of love, which ye have shewed toward his name, in that ye have ministered to the saints, and do minister.
>
> And we desire that every one of you do shew the same diligence to the full assurance of hope unto the end:
>
> That ye be not slothful, but followers of them who through faith and patience inherit the promises.
>
> For when God made promise to Abraham, because he could swear by no greater, he sware by himself,
>
> Saying, Surely blessing I will bless thee, and multiplying I will multiply thee.
>
> And so, after he had patiently endured, he obtained the promise. (Hebrews 6:7–15)

God's purpose for giving this entire section is to present a contrast between the actions and fruit-bearing of those who are truly committed to the Lord and those who are merely dabblers and pretenders, like Judas. In verse 7, God compares the genuine believer to a plot of land upon the earth. He says that the land received certain provisions that would enable it to bring forth a kind of fruit that would benefit the one who dressed it. The fruit was befitting of the investment bestowed upon it by the husbandman who worked it.

He pronounces a blessing upon this type of ground. The parallel is, of course, a man or woman who has received the benefit of certain ministries from the Lord and has responded accordingly, producing fruit that is befitting of the ministry received and will benefit the Lord, who bestowed the labor, as a husbandman (John 15:1).

In verse 8, He provides the contrast that represents the dabbler's response to the ministry of the Word and the Spirit in his life. He receives the same provisions, but his fruit represents an accursed response. He does not produce a fruit that is befitting of (meet for) the ministry he has received and that benefits the One giving the provision.

This plot of land is rejected and nigh unto cursing. Jesus said in John 15:16 that He had chosen His disciples with a purpose in mind: that they bear fruit and that their fruit would remain. ALL MEN have received the ministry of the light that came into the world and enlightened every man (John 1:4–5, 9).

> In him was life; and the life was the light
> of men.
> And the light shineth in darkness; and the
> darkness comprehended it not. (John 1:4–5)

> That was the true Light, which lighteth
> every man that cometh into the world. (John 1:9)

THE RESPONSE OF MEN TO THE LIGHT DETERMINES THEIR DESTINY. Most reject the Light outright because of their love for their sin, according to John 3:16–21. There is a second group found in Hebrews 6:4–6 and 6:8, which dabbles with the faith but never fully commits to it. These are the ones that the text of Hebrews 5:11–6:15 is seeking to warn. God wants them to get off the fence and quit hanging around the perimeter, but to come down on the side of full commitment.

The third group, which Hebrews 6:7 is speaking about, represents the majority of Paul's audience, as he alludes to in Hebrews 6:9. These are the ones that prove the reality of their faith/walk with Jesus by the FRUIT they BEAR. Hebrews 6:9 is KEY to the passage.

Paul is pointing out that there are some legitimate proofs of one's salvation. He is taking the pulse, so to speak, of many who say they are followers of Christ but who actually do not manifest THE THINGS THAT ACCOMPANY SALVATION. This context is a warning to all to examine themselves to see whether they are in the faith or not by looking for the appropriate fruits, as he exhorts the Corinthians to do in 2 Corinthians 13:5.

It is NOT teaching that someone can be legitimately saved and later fall away from that blessed state. Rather, "By THEIR FRUITS ye shall know them" (Matthew 7:15–20). In Hebrews 6:10, God points to the FRUIT that He is looking for in every truly committed follower.

He says that He will not forget the things that they have done for the saints out of their love for Jesus Christ. He assures them that it would be unrighteous for Him to do so. He also points to the fact that the continuation of the work of ministering to the saints out of their love for God is a validating proof of the third group's being genuinely saved. In Hebrews 6:11, God tells every individual who wants to consider himself or herself to be a genuine follower of Jesus Christ to manifest the same diligent service and to bear the same good fruit that those commended previously have been bearing and to do so unto the end. In Hebrews 6:12, He tells them to avoid slothfulness by following those who through faith and patience inherited His promises.

It is so easy to follow God for a little while, but the majority of people do not have the faith and patience to follow through the long periods of waiting on God that often precede the fulfillment of those promises. That is one of the biggest reasons most professing believers end up falling away. They are among the impatient dabblers who have never committed themselves to FOLLOWING GOD FOR THE DURATION: no matter what comes and no matter how long it takes to be found in the place of obedience until the blessing comes.

Consider the story of Elisha when the time had come for Elijah to be carried up into heaven in 2 Kings 2:1–15.

God planned to bless Elisha with his requested double portion of the Spirit that rested upon Elijah if he was around to SEE the miracle of Elijah being carried up into heaven. He was given multiple opportunities to take a break and BE OUT OF HIS PLACE BESIDE ELIJAH, but he REFUSED each opportunity to relax his pursuit of God and take a leave of absence from his service to Elijah. He was not at first aware of the condition God had set upon his request. He had not at first been given the offer of making his request, and if he had taken leave from his place of service, he would have never received the offer from God through Elijah or the blessing that God had for him by being IN HIS PLACE.

So many people today MISS OUT on the BEST that God has FOR them because they are always taking leave from the place of OBEDIENCE and SERVICE that they are supposed to continually occupy. God tells us in Hebrews 6:11–12 to REMAIN STEADFAST and UNMOVABLE and, in essence, to always be abounding in the work of the Lord until the end comes. In Hebrews 6:13–15, God gives the example of Abraham and how he believed God's promise and continued to serve God faithfully and with much patience over the many years between the time that the promise of God was given and the time when he finally received the actual fulfillment of that promise. For the true child of God, there CAN NEVER BE A DAY when our faith gives up and walks away from Him and His promises.

IN THAT is manifested the true child of God. Now LET'S LOOK AT THAT CONTEXT AGAIN WITH FRESH EYES.

> Of whom (Christ Melchisedec) we have
> many things to say, and hard to be uttered, seeing
> ye are dull of hearing. (Hebrews 5:11)

Paul complains here that there are many additional things that he needs to teach his hearers, but he can't because their eyes have glazed over, and what is being said is going in one ear and out the other. He says, "It's like you are half asleep and not really listening in an active manner. It's hard to teach you anything because you're not REALLY paying attention. You are like the teenager that says, 'Yeah, yeah, I know. I know,' but you really don't get it."

> For when for the time ye ought to be teach-
> ers, ye have need that one teach you again which
> be the first principles of the oracles of God; and

> are become such as have need of milk, and not of
> strong meat. (Hebrews 5:12)

Paul is declaring that they have already heard enough to be able to be teachers themselves. He is stating that God has the expectation that TRUE disciples GROW UP SPIRITUALLY and become teachers themselves of the basic doctrines once they have heard them and have begun to put them into practice in their lives. His complaint is that some of his hearers have never put into practice the things they have already been taught and need to hear the same basic baby food teachings over and over again. He tells them that they can't receive the MEAT OF THE WORD because they have not really received and assimilated the BABY FOOD messages they have already heard.

> For every one that useth milk is unskillful
> in the word of righteousness: for he is a babe.
> (Hebrews 5:13)

He is saying that milk is for babies, but God EXPECTS that ALL BABIES GROW UP and become fully functioning adults. The question that he develops in this context is: Are you truly born again? His assertion is that IF YOU ARE, then CERTAIN THINGS WILL ACCOMPANY THAT SALVATION (Hebrews 6:9).

He is saying to some that either they are stunted in their growth or they are not truly one of Christ's own. He says that for some, he is looking for a pulse of sorts as a sign of life, and he is not finding one. What he is seeing in some is an indication that they may have never fully taken the plunge and committed themselves to the Lord.

> But strong meat belongeth to them that are
> of full age, even those who by reason of use have
> their senses exercised to discern both good and
> evil. (Hebrews 5:14)

Paul is saying that you won't be able to receive the weightier principles of God's Word until you have exercised the spiritual sense that God has already bestowed through the basics of the Word BY PUTTING INTO PRACTICE what you already know. The entire tenor of these verses in chapter 5 is to convey God's expectation that His true followers should GO ON TO GROW UP, so they can become a part of the teaching ministry of their local church and bear fruit in the lives of others, instead of always needing to be on the receiving end of ministry.

> Therefore leaving the principles of the doctrine of Christ, let us go on unto perfection; not laying again the foundation of repentance from dead works, and of faith toward God,
> Of the doctrine of baptisms, and of laying on of hands, and of resurrection of the dead, and of eternal judgment. (Hebrews 6:1–2)

He is saying, "Don't make me have to go over the same basic lesson plan over and over and over. You have heard about who Jesus is. You have been told that you must repent and turn away from your old lifestyle and put your faith in the Lord.

YOU KNOW ALL OF THAT! You have heard about baptism and the laying on of hands. You have heard all about the resurrection and eternal judgment. So let's MOVE ON! Don't make me have to repeat myself OVER and OVER. Let us GO ON TO PERFECTION (or grow up into Christian maturity)."

> And this will we do, if God permit.
> (Hebrews 6:3)

This is one of the scariest verses in the Bible. Spiritual life is given when God takes the holy seed of the WORD of God and waters it with the HOLY SPIRIT, and the seed germinates, and the man is BORN AGAIN. That is what John spoke of in chapter 3 and Paul spoke about in Titus chapter 3. Peter refers to it in 1 Peter 1:23. The mystery of this wondrous work of grace is that in some mysterious way, God works within the free will of man to produce this new birth. He does NOT FORCE Himself upon anyone. There is a sense in which NO MAN CAN COME TO JESUS for salvation UNLESS the FATHER DRAWS him (John 6:65). There is another sense in which THE CROSS OF JESUS DRAWS ALL MEN TO HIM (John 12:32). Jesus has brought the light of salvation into the world, and every man has been a partaker of that light (John 1:9; 3:16–21).

There are many who follow Jesus for a time, but for the wrong reasons (John 6:26). Those followers are NOT TRUE BELIEVERS, possessing the QUALITY OF FAITH THAT SAVES (John 6:60; 64–66).

They hang around the perimeter and often pass for true disciples, but eventually hear something over which THEY CHOKE—something they cannot swallow—and then they often decide to walk away from the Lord. Much like Job was tempted to do by the determined efforts of Satan (Job 1:11; 2:5, 9). God will present the light to man. God will use the message of the cross to draw men to Jesus, but He won't force men to be saved. He has done everything necessary to save the souls of men, BUT HE WILL NOT PERMIT THEM TO BE SAVED UNLESS THEY WILLINGLY RECEIVE HIS COMMAND TO REPENT (Acts 17:30; 2 Timothy 2:24–26; Luke 13:3, 5).

> For it is impossible for those who were once enlightened, and have tasted of the heavenly gift, and were made partakers of the Holy Ghost,
> And have tasted the good word of God, and the powers of the world to come. (Hebrews 6:4–5)

It has already been demonstrated from John 1:9 and 3:16–21 that man can be enlightened but not come to that true Light in a saving manner. Anyone can taste but not swallow the heavenly gift, the good Word of God, and the powers of the world to come. Everyone who hears the Word of truth has the Holy Spirit bear witness to that truth, so everyone in that sense is a partaker of the Holy Ghost, but that doesn't necessarily mean that they RECEIVE THE HOLY SPIRIT'S CORRECTION. When Stephen preached in Acts 7:51–60, he was full of the Holy Ghost and preached a message telling the people that they always resist the Holy Ghost, and they stoned him to death. NONE OF THESE STATEMENTS PROVE THE PEOPLE HE IS WARNING WERE SAVED.

In fact, the overall context strongly argues that the ones he is warning were not truly saved, like those we just mentioned in John 6:66.

> If they shall fall away, to renew them again
> unto repentance; seeing they crucify to them-
> selves the Son of God afresh, and put him to an
> open shame. (Hebrews 6:6)

I MUST BEGIN the examination of this verse with the observation that virtually every group that believes that a person can LOSE his or her salvation will USE THIS VERSE to validate their teaching. However, those same groups virtually all believe that IF you do happen to LOSE your salvation, you can be saved again. However, if this verse teaches that one can lose his salvation, then IT ALSO TEACHES that YOU CAN NEVER GET IT BACK AGAIN! Look at what it says IN ITS CONTEXT, which includes the following:

> FOR IT IS IMPOSSIBLE. IF they shall FALL
> AWAY, TO RENEW THEM AGAIN UNTO REPEN-
> TANCE. (Hebrews 6:4)

Isn't it interesting that they never put two and two together, but they pick and choose what they want and ignore the rest of the context when they are trying to prove their points? We should be like Samuel and Eli in the Old Testament. Samuel said, "Speak, for Thy servant heareth" (1 Samuel 3:10). Then Eli, when he was inquiring of Samuel what God had spoken to him, said, "What is the thing that the LORD hath said unto thee? I pray thee hide it not from me: God do so to thee, and more also, if thou hide anything from me of all the things that He said unto thee" (1 Samuel 3:17).

WHAT IS GOD SAYING IN THIS OVERALL CONTEXT?

He is saying that, IF someone is A DABBLER and not a committed follower of the Lord Jesus Christ, he can be a partaker of many of the benefits that HE came to give to the world without FULLY SWALLOWING the MESSAGE and becoming a fully devoted follower of Jesus Christ. IF they play around the edges and follow Jesus the way the multitude did in John chapter 6 and Judas did for the entire three and a half years, then once they make a decision to walk away, they will not return again, just like they did in John 6.

This whole section is AN EXTREME WARNING that God expects His TRUE children to go on to perfection and become teachers themselves of others, but that if someone is not really committed, they may look like a stalk of wheat for a while, but they may eventually walk away and reveal themselves to be a TARE instead. The Bible tells us that our hearts are deceitful above all things and desperately wicked (Jeremiah 17:9).

The Bible speaks about the deceitfulness of sin. The Bible speaks about an adversary called the devil, who is a deceiver and the father of lies. Paul said that we need to examine ourselves and prove our own selves to see whether or not we are truly IN THE FAITH. John says:

> They went out from us, but they were not
> of us; for if they had been of us, they would no
> doubt have continued with us: but they went out,
> that they might be made manifest that they were
> not all of us. (1 John 2:19)

In John 6, there was a multitude that followed Jesus and seemed to be His disciples, but they never really were. He spoke to them WORDS that were SPIRIT and LIFE and said, "Except ye eat the flesh of the Son of man, and drink His blood, ye have no life in you." The multitude said, "This is a hard saying. Who can hear it?" Then it says, "From that time many of His disciples went back, and walked no more with Him" (John 6:66). Ultimately, Jesus was telling the multitude that they had to SWALLOW the idea of His broken body and shed blood as being their ONLY HOPE of going to heaven when they died.

That is the essence of the spiritual message that His Words were conveying. Because they were followers on the perimeter and not fully committed, like Peter, who spoke for eleven of the apostles, they fell away and walked no more with Jesus. They never came back. Peter said:

> Lord, to whom shall we go? thou hast the
> words of eternal life. And we believe and are sure
> that thou art that Christ, the Son of the living
> God. (John 6:68–69)

For the fully devoted follower of Jesus Christ, THERE IS NO TURNING BACK! There is no walking away! For the individual that CAN walk away, there never was TRUE SALVATION in the first place. They don't obtain it truly because they are not truly committed to Him in the first place. It says in John 6 that Jesus "knew from the beginning who they were that believed not" (John 6:64).

The multitude NEVER WERE TRUE DISCIPLES, so they could walk away.

Now we just finished alluding to a principle above from Jeremiah 17:9 that creates a great segue into a discussion of the next section of Scripture that is so often misunderstood by folks who have been taught that one can be genuinely saved and then later so grievously sin or so deliberately walk away from Christ as to forfeit or lose the salvation once formerly obtained. ANOTHER MAJOR PASSAGE THAT CAUSES DOUBT IS Hebrews 10:23–31.

> Let us hold fast the profession of our
> faith without wavering; (for he is faithful that
> promised;)
> And let us consider one another to provoke
> unto love and to good works:
> Not forsaking the assembling of ourselves
> together, as the manner of some is; but exhorting

one another: and so much the more, as ye see the day approaching.

For if we sin willfully after that we have received the knowledge of the truth, there remaineth no more sacrifice for sins,

But a certain fearful looking for of judgment and fiery indignation, which shall devour the adversaries.

He that despised Moses' law died without mercy under two or three witnesses:

Of how much sorer punishment, suppose ye, shall he be thought worthy, who hath trodden under foot the Son of God, and hath counted the blood of the covenant, wherewith he was sanctified, an unholy thing, and hath done despite unto the Spirit of grace?

For we know him that hath said, Vengeance belongeth unto me, I will recompense, saith the Lord. And again, The Lord shall judge his people.

It is a fearful thing to fall into the hands of the living God. (Hebrews 10:23–31)

The verses above have been confusing to many souls over the years and have served as a basis for the belief that God's people can fail to hold on to their profession of faith and carelessly fall into willful sin in such a way as to cause God to vengefully recompense them in judgment by withdrawing His mercy and presumably stripping away their salvation.

It is the cause of great concern to many sincere souls because of that conclusion, and it is looked upon as a great warning that man needs to fiercely hold on to his profession of faith lest he lose his salvation altogether because of such above-described carelessness.

The words in the text above are the main focus of this point of view, and the main concern is based on the idea that God is directing the warning toward His own people, as is stated in verse 30: "The Lord shall judge his people."

I think that the best way to begin the examination of this interpretation of the Scriptures above is to acknowledge that there is a very serious warning that is being conveyed and that the seriousness of the said warning should cause every serious Bible student to sit up and take notice of what is being said. Then as is so often the case, it is best to read the entire chapter and not just the passage in question to gain an understanding of the meaning within the larger context. When that is done carefully, the emphasis of the warning turns away from a warning to God's people about the potential of their losing their salvation to a warning to God's people to consider others on the perimeter of the faith and to live in such a way as to continually serve as a provocation to the uncommitted to get off the fence and quit playing around because they are all approaching a line of demarcation in time, when it will be too late to make the choice for Christ.

The true children of God are to so live that they will be constantly stirring the heart of the *five foolish virgins* as it were to WISE UP: to recognize by the example being set before them by the true children of God that there is something missing in their connection with God that needs to be addressed before it is too late!

Given the FACT that the heart of man is deceitful above all things and desperately wicked, as it says in Jeremiah 17:9, the true child of God is to realize that many professing Christians are not truly children of God after all, BUT THEY BELIEVE THAT THEY ARE, and they are being deceived by their own hearts. For that reason, the true children of God are commanded to do SIX things:

1. Draw near with a true heart in full assurance of faith, having our hearts sprinkled from an evil conscience, and our bodies washed with pure water.
2. Hold fast to the profession of our faith without wavering.
3. Consider one another.
4. Provoke (one another) unto love and (unto) good works.
5. NOT FORSAKE THE ASSEMBLING OF OURSELVES TOGETHER.
6. Exhort one another more and more as we see the day of Christ's return approaching.

Now just as Romans 9:6–8 makes a distinction between the generic and the true Israel, the judgment of God, which must BEGIN at the house of God according to 1 Peter 4:17, will also make a distinction between the wheat and the tares among those who claim to be the children of God within the house of God.

That is why the true child of God is charged with considering and provoking everyone by their continuing and even increasing assembling together to accomplish that task!

The five foolish virgins in Matthew 25 all assumed that they were as ready as the five wise virgins for the Lord's return, but they were wrong. They would no doubt be among the multitude on the Day of Judgment who say: "Have we not prophesied in thy name? And in thy name have cast out devils? and in thy name done many wonderful works?" Yet Jesus states that He never knew them in Matthew 7:22–23! Hebrews 10 is not talking about the true people of God losing their salvation. Rather, it is talking again about the dabblers who THINK they are saved, and their need to be stirred up and provoked by the example of the true children of God, lest they fall away, as so many are doing today and have done in the past. Chapter 10 begins by discussing the eternal perfecting of the truly saved by the one-time sacrifice of Jesus Christ as a better and permanent offering for sins.

His sacrifice forever purges the conscience of sins. He by the one offering sanctifies the believing sinner once and for all. The offering of Jesus not only purges the sinners' consciences but ERASES THE MEMORY OF GOD CONCERNING THE GUILT OF THEIR SIN!

> And their sins and their iniquities will I
> remember no more. (Hebrews 10:17)

Verses 18–25 begin one of the most beautiful and significant sections in the Bible.

All through chapter 9 the Lord discusses the tabernacle and the holy place and how only the High Priest could enter into the presence of God and even he could only enter once a year and not without blood. He explains how Jesus provided a different kind of offering than all of the high priests in the past had offered every year. Every year, they were reminded of their sins and the sins of the people because of the very nature of the animal sacrifices instituted under the old covenant. Christ's offering was different and far better. It provided a one-time eternal sacrifice that perfected the sinner, purged his conscience, erased the memory of god with regard to the believer's sin, and provided A NEW WAY INTO THE HOLIEST (the holy place in the temple of God in heaven). Through the veil, that is to say, His flesh and now, invites His children to come boldly into His presence (Hebrews 4:12–16).

Unlike the access offered to any of the Old Testament prophets (with the exception of Moses), priests, and kings, God says in essence: in light of the hitherto undreamed of access into my presence for the true child of God that no one had in the Old Testament, I command you to draw near, hold fast, consider one another, and provoke one another to love and do good works, not to forsake the assembly, but to exhort one another more and more BECAUSE if a man can walk away he has nothing more that can be done on his behalf to make an offering for his sin.

He has nothing more to look forward to than judgment and fiery indignation, which shall devour the adversaries. There is nothing that even hints at the idea that a genuinely saved person, described in verses 1–17, could ever or would ever even seriously consider walking away from the privilege that we have been afforded in Christ is described in verses 18–21.

To whom would we go? How else could our sins be completely paid for? How else could our conscience be purged of the sense of our guilt for all of our sins? How else could God's memory of our guilt be erased but through Jesus? How else could we have the hitherto undreamed-of access that we have into our father's presence that even King David, a man after God's own heart, was denied in the old testament? To put things simply, God is warning the church about the people that need to be provoked and exhorted and have a continual example set for them of what a true child of God looks like and is supposed to be and act like to no doubt manifest contrast with what they can see in their own life and reveal that their own heart has deceived them into believing they are saved when they in fact are not.

The warning is that if we don't reach them before it is too late, there is nothing more that can be done for them. It is our duty to HIM to try to reach them, and we can't do it by the hit-and-miss inconsistency of most professing believers. It makes one wonder how many are in fact truly saved among the multitude that profess to be. Now look at the remainder of the chapter from verse 32 and on to the end. God is telling everyone of His followers to remember the suffering that they endured at the beginning of their journey and to "embrace the grind" as some people have said in other contexts. He tells His audience that there is a great reward for continuing on in THE FAITH and that no one will profit if he or she casts off that faith. Then He assures the reader that patience will be rewarded at His coming and warns that He will have no pleasure in someone drawing back into unbelief and perdition. Lastly, He defines the quality of THE FAITH THAT PRODUCES SALVATION as being a faith that never does turn back but remains to the end.

Hence, AGAIN IF A MAN CAN WALK AWAY FROM HIS FAITH, HE WAS NEVER SAVED IN THE FIRST PLACE! Read all of chapters 9 and 10, and you will understand the contrasts between the old covenant and the new one. You will see the contrast between the Old Testament high priest and Jesus. You will see the contrast between the Old Testament sacrifices and the one that Jesus offered. You will notice a difference between the yearly and even daily ritual offerings and how the offering of Jesus completely fulfilled all the types and finally fully satisfied the judgment of God and thus made the true children of God completely forgiven and eternally sanctified. You will also see that God has had His memory of our sins erased. Also, by comparing Hebrews 9 and 10 with the Gospels, where the veil in the temple was rent in twain from the top to the bottom, you will see that the way into the holiest was made through that veil that is to say His flesh BY that "ONE OFFERING" for sin. Additionally, for those who have been taught that IF one can actually lose his or her salvation he or she can get saved again, let me point out very clearly what is said in Hebrews

10. Hebrews 10:18 Now where remission of these is, there is no more offering for sin.

> For if we sin willfully after that we have received the knowledge of the truth, there remaineth no more sacrifice for sins,
>
> But a certain fearful looking for of judgment and fiery indignation, which shall devour the adversaries. (Hebrews 10:26–27)

Here is the problem, and it is a HUGE problem! IF you could get saved and later lose your salvation, there would be NO MORE OFFERING FOR SIN. You would have already "trodden under foot the Son of God," so you would not be able to get saved again!

IF you insist on interpreting what God is saying in that way, you are stuck with the rest of what goes along with that interpretation, and frankly WHO WANTS THAT? But you have no choice! If God is saying that genuinely saved people can lose their salvation, then He is also saying that they CANNOT GET SAVED AGAIN, because they have rejected the offering of Jesus Christ, and there IS NO MORE OFFERING for them to bring to God.

> He that despised Moses' law died without mercy under two or three witnesses:
>
> Of how much sorer punishment, suppose ye, shall he be thought worthy, who hath trodden under foot the Son of God, and hath counted the blood of the covenant, wherewith he was sanctified, an unholy thing, and hath done despite unto the Spirit of grace? (Hebrews 10:28–29)

If you cross that line of walking away, you must step over and tread underfoot the outstretched hand of Jesus Christ as He pleads for you, "Father forgive them, for they know not what they do." Once you do that, there is "no more offering for sin." Once you spit in the face of the Spirit of Grace that offers, "For by grace are ye saved through faith. It is the gift of God, there remaineth no more offering for sins, but a certain fearful looking for of judgment and of fiery indignation, which shall devour the adversaries." I declare unto you most assuredly that IF you can lose your salvation, you can NEVER BE SAVED AGAIN!

A THIRD PASSAGE THAT CAUSES CONCERN IS THIS:

> He that overcometh, the same shall be clothed in white raiment; and I will not blot out his name out of the book of life, but I will confess his name before my Father, and before his angels. (Revelation 3:5)

The concern for many is that somehow a person can get saved, get his name written in the Book of Life, and later have his or her name removed or blotted out. The idea is that if one's name is blotted out of the Book of Life, that person will be eternally lost after being saved at an earlier date. However, it will be good for anyone who thinks that way to consider several things.

The Book of Life is only mentioned eight times in the whole Bible. All of those times with the exception of one are found in the book of Revelation.

- Philippians 4:3
- Revelation 3:5
- Revelation 13:8
- Revelation 17:8
- Revelation 20:12
- Revelation 20:15
- Revelation 21:7
- Revelation 22:19

It may also be referred to in Exodus 32:32–33.

1. The Bible does not actually say when a person's name is placed in the Book of Life. The assumption on the part of many is that your name is added to the Lamb's Book of Life after a person gets saved, and if that were true, it would indicate that one could lose salvation after obtaining it if his or her name were later blotted out of the book. HOWEVER,

2. If every person who has ever lived had their name written in His book when He created them, OR even before the foundation of the world (Revelation 17:8) because He knew He would create them, then the only thing that matters is to make sure our name does not get blotted out of the book.

3. We have to be careful not to add to the Words of God OR to take away from them, lest we run into the problems God pronounces upon those who do.

> For I testify unto every man that heareth the words of the prophecy of this book, If any man shall add unto these things, God shall add unto him the plagues that are written in this book:
>
> And if any man shall take away from the words of the book of this prophecy, God shall take away his part out of the book of life, and out of the holy city, and from the things which are written in this book. (Revelation 22:18–19)

4. The only way to get any of the verses that describe the Book of Life to teach that one can lose his salvation is to add to His word what He doesn't actually say: that our name is ADDED to the Book of Life after we get saved. We must also take away from His Word in the verses that deal with Him giving His sheep in this life the gift of eternal life and the promises that those who possess eternal life will

never perish, neither will any man pluck us out of His hand and His Father's hands.

So again, we find the scriptures used to teach that one can lose his or her salvation to be actually teaching the exact opposite.

5. Virtually every time a verse or group of verses is found to be confusing and to seem to imply that a saved person can lose his or her salvation, they will be found to be merely describing the characteristics of someone who was never truly saved, but was one of the tares, like Judas and those described in 1 John 2:19.

6. Remember again, His sheep hear His voice and FOLLOW HIM!

ANOTHER PASSAGE THAT TROUBLES A LOT OF FOLKS IS THIS:

Christ is become of no effect unto you, whosoever of you are justified by the law; ye are fallen from grace. (Galatians 5:4)

The thought for some from this verse is that a person has fallen from a state of grace and that he or she has lost his or her salvation accordingly. They usually couple this verse with Hebrews 6:6, which says: "IF they shall FALL AWAY..." and conclude that a person can be genuinely saved at one point and later fall away from that place of salvation. However, the entire book of Galatians is written to establish unequivocally the fact that a man's salvation is not based on his performance, but on the grace of Christ and His work on our behalf alone.

Remember, Paul had founded churches in Galatia based on his message of the grace of God through faith. After his departure from the area, as he proceeded on his missionary journey, he got word from some messengers that the Judaizers (a group of Jewish believers still determined to bring Gentiles under the Law, even after they had professed faith in Christ) had come behind him to Galatia and had begun teaching that the believers in Christ still had to be circumcised and keep the Law of Moses to be saved. They were thus adding to the Word of God that Paul had preached to the churches of Galatia, and the book of Galatians was God's reply. Paul says that he marvels that they had been so soon removed from the Holy Spirit's message of grace that he had preached and that they had begun to embrace what amounted to another gospel and another Christ.

> I marvel that ye are so soon removed from
> him that called you into the grace of Christ unto
> another gospel. (Galatians 1:6)

He pronounces a curse on anyone who preaches another gospel.

> But though we, or an angel from heaven,
> preach any other gospel unto you than that which
> we have preached unto you, let him be accursed.
> (Galatians 1:8)

In the remainder of chapter 1, Paul testifies to his credentials and to the fact that his message was directly from haven and not from man. In chapter 2, he details the work that he had done spreading the gospel and the debate that had arisen with the Judaizers over whether or not the Gentile converts needed to be circumcised and observe the Law of Moses and how the question had been resolved when he had taken the matter to the leadership in Jerusalem. Then he discusses the fact that Peter had even been caught up in the controversy while they were together in Antioch and needed to be corrected. He stated that men need to understand that if they were planning to approach God on the basis of the works of the Law, they had better be prepared to be perfect.

On the other hand, if they planned to approach God on the basis of the grace of God through Jesus, they needed to realize that there was no mixing law and grace. It was either one or the other. The fact that no one is perfect under the Law requires that ALL come to God through GRACE ALONE.

In chapter 3, he accuses the Galatians of having fallen under a bewitching spell that had caused them to not obey the truth of the gospel of Christ. He reminds them of their initial struggles and how the Holy Spirit had worked in their midst. He asks them if they believe that the miracles performed were God's response to their works or their faith. He reminds them of Abraham and how his life was a testimony to faith and trust in God, and that is how he found favor with God, rather than by his own works of righteousness. He points out that the Law was only a schoolmaster to bring them to Jesus, but that after it had accomplished its purpose, believers were no longer to be in bondage under its weight.

In chapter 4, Paul asserts that the child of God has a higher heritage under grace than under the Law and that believers have ascended from the position of servants under the Law to sons under grace. Our inheritance under grace, like that of Isaac, is higher than our position as a servant under the Law, like that of Ishmael. Paul argues that he is concerned over the Galatians' gravitation toward falling back under the Law, which is a lower place, as that of a servant, instead of that of a son. Grace is a higher place to be under than the Law. Would you rather be Hagar or Sarah? Would you rather be the son of promise, Isaac, or the son of a bond servant, Ishmael? Would you rather be in bondage OR BE FREE?

Paul says that he stands in doubt about some of them, in essence wondering if somehow they had missed out on the whole benefit of his ministry among them and if some of them were possibly never really saved after all. In chapter 5, Paul begins to summarize his argument and bring it toward a place of invitation to a decision. He tells them to stand fast in the liberty of Christ and not be entangled again in the yoke of bondage. He tells them that IF they seek to be justified by the Law and by being circumcised, Christ will not profit them at all. He tells them that the new doctrine that some were entertaining did not come from the Lord, who had called them to Himself and salvation by His grace. He tells them that IF they choose to continue on they would be falling from the high place of freedom and the blessing of sonship under grace to a lower place of bondage under the Law.

His point is: WHY SETTLE FOR THAT WHEN GOD HAS PROVIDED FOR THIS? THIS IS BETTER! He is not saying that someone, who is genuinely saved, can fall from a state of grace and lose their salvation. His message is TWOFOLD. First, he is saying that salvation is not obtained under the Law because no one is perfect, so if you are looking to be justified under the Law, what Christ did for you will not apply, and you are out of luck.

If you somehow missed the message in the past and were unclear about that, NOW IS THE TIME TO PUT YOUR FAITH IN JESUS CHRIST, but realize that if you are purposing to choose the Law over grace as your means of being justified in the sight of God, you have chosen a lower heritage that will not end up profiting you at all. ANOTHER FASCINATING SECTION THAT IS CONFUSING IS AS FOLLOWS:

> Take heed, brethren, lest there be in any of
> you an evil heart of unbelief, in departing from
> the living God.
> But exhort one another daily, while it
> is called To day; lest any of you be hardened
> through the deceitfulness of sin.
> For we are made partakers of Christ, if we
> hold the beginning of our confidence steadfast
> unto the end. (Hebrews 3:12–14)

The reasoning here should be pretty obvious to anyone who reads it. The thought is that, first, we will only be able to be saved (a partaker of Christ) if we hold on to our faith in Him all the way to the end. The reasoning is that if we start out in faith but then depart in unbelief, then we lose our salvation—assuming, of course, that our faith got us saved in the first place and made us at least potentially a partaker of Christ until we later decide to turn back and walk away. This reasoning is sound to a certain degree, except that interpreting it that way would create a contradiction to some of those clearly stated passages.

Since one of the first principles of hermeneutics states that there can be no genuine contradictions in the Bible, this passage forces us to go back and ask: WHICH PASSAGE IS CLEARER WHEN IT COMES TO THE QUESTION OF SALVATION? This one or John 10:27–30 and John 3:16–18, for instance?

1. John 3:16–18 is clearly discussing the question of salvation, as we look back at the beginning of the chapter and the Lord's discussion of being born again with Nicodemus. The context is clearly talking about being born again or being saved. The language is clear.
2. John 10:27–30 is clearly discusses how an individual gets into Heaven, comparing Jesus to the door into the dwelling place of the Father or at least into the sheepfold, as it were. He talks about thieves trying to "climb up some other way." Climb up to where? The implication is to Heaven. Without listing the entire chapter here, I would refer the reader to the verses themselves in the Bible to verify that the context is talking about how to be saved.
3. Hebrews 3:12–14 is actually in a context that describes a SECOND REST. It is not necessarily talking about salvation. Consider the entirety of the context of the chapter and consider its parallel in the following:

> The thief cometh not, but for to steal, and to kill, and to destroy: I am come that they might have life, and that they might have it more abundantly. (John 10:10)

Jesus states that his coming had a TWOFOLD PURPOSE:

1. To provide LIFE (the ETERNAL LIFE OF GOD), so we could label that salvation. We were dead in trespasses and sins, and God quickened us together with Christ according to Ephesians 2:1–4.
2. To provide life MORE ABUNDANTLY. This is BEYOND MERE SALVATION. It is an overflowing, victorious life. It is the best

life. It is the life that God has planned for us in accordance with Jeremiah 29:11.

> For I know the thoughts that I think toward
> you, saith the LORD, thoughts of peace, and not
> of evil, to give you an expected end. (Jeremiah
> 29:11)

It is David's experience with the Good Shepherd in Psalm 23.

> My cup runneth over. Surely goodness and
> mercy shall follow me all the days of my life: and
> I will dwell in the house of the LORD for ever.
> (Psalm 23:5–6)

In Hebrews 3 and 4, the subject God is discussing is what many theologians call the *second rest*.

> There remaineth therefore a rest to the peo-
> ple of God.
> For he that is entered into his rest, he also
> hath ceased from his own works, as God did
> from his.
> Let us labour therefore to enter into that
> rest, lest any man fall after the same example of
> unbelief. (Hebrews 4:9–11)

Notice: There remaineth therefore a rest to the people of God. This is a yet-to-be-realized rest beyond salvation. It is one from which the Old Testament saints who came out of Egypt with Moses were excluded because of their unbelief. The New Testament child of God is warned here in the book of Hebrews, chapters 3 and 4, to not fol-low after the same example of unbelief that characterized the people of God in the Old Testament and kept them out of the Promised

Land. Simply put, they had faith to GET OUT of Egypt, but they did not have the faith necessary to GET INTO the Promised Land.

> Wherefore I was grieved with that generation, and said, They do alway err in their heart; and they have not known my ways.
> So I sware in my wrath, They shall not enter into my rest. (Hebrews 3:10–11)

Consider the TWOFOLD NATURE of the Lord's intended will for His people.

> Ye shall diligently keep the commandments of the LORD your God, and his testimonies, and his statutes, which he hath commanded thee.
> And thou shalt do that which is right and good in the sight of the LORD: that it may be well with thee, and that thou mayest go in and possess the good land which the LORD sware unto thy fathers,
> To cast out all thine enemies from before thee, as the LORD hath spoken.
> And when thy son asketh thee in time to come, saying, What mean the testimonies, and the statutes, and the judgments, which the LORD our God hath commanded you?
> Then thou shalt say unto thy son, We were Pharaoh's bondmen in Egypt; and the LORD brought us out of Egypt with a mighty hand:
> And the LORD shewed signs and wonders, great and sore, upon Egypt, upon Pharaoh, and upon all his household, before our eyes:
> And he brought us out from thence, that he might bring us in, to give us the land which he sware unto our fathers.

> And the L**ORD** commanded us to do all
> these statutes, to fear the L**ORD** our God, for our
> good always, that he might preserve us alive, as it
> is at this day. (Deuteronomy 6:17–24)

His plan is to FIRST bring us OUT from under our bondage to Egypt (the world) to bring us unto Himself THAT He might BRING US INTO THE PROMISED LAND (Canaan for the Old Testament Jews) of the ABUNDANT LIFE in the New Testament.

He brought Israel out from their bondage to slavery in Egypt, and He gave them the FIRST rest. LATER, when He would have brought them into the Promised Land, they could not enter because of their unbelief, so the Lord sware in His wrath that they would not enter into His rest (the SECOND REST), wherein they would have inherited houses they did not build and vineyards they did not plant and many other blessings the Lord had in store for them.

Read the whole story in Numbers 13–14.

The warning in Hebrews

Chapters 3 and 4 convey that there is something very special beyond the first rest that we as New Testament believers can miss out on if we are not careful. Receiving the first rest is no guarantee that we will enter into the second rest. With those things being said, let's look again at chapters 3 and 4 in Hebrews.

In Hebrews 3:1–2, the exhortation is given to "Consider the Apostle and High Priest of our profession, Christ Jesus, who was faithful to Him that appointed Him." Chapter 4 ends with the admonition to consider Him and the access we have through Him unto the throne of grace, where we can find mercy and grace to help us in our times of need. He is a faithful High Priest who understands our infirmities and bids us to come unto Him.

Chapter 2 tells us that He is able to "succour" (comfort, help, relieve) us because He can understand and identify with us and our infirmities and temptations. Chapter 4 also makes the same claims. In the midst of those truths, we are told to follow through with Jesus to lay hold of all that He has for our lives and the rest that He has available for us.

These things are the main thrust of the chapters. If we take verses out of their context, the main focus can seem to change, and the resultant interpretation can thus be skewed (twisted to a change of direction). In Hebrews 3:6 and 3:14, we have two very brief statements that taken by themselves may be interpreted as speaking about our initial salvation from the condemnation of sin and its attendant punishment in hell.

> But Christ as a son over his own house; whose house are we, if we hold fast the confidence and the rejoicing of the hope firm unto the end. (Hebrews 3:6)

> For we are made partakers of Christ, if we hold the beginning of our confidence steadfast unto the end. (Hebrews 3:14)

However, the rest of chapters 3 and 4 actually discuss the ABUNDANT LIFE, rather than the LIFE (John 10:10). When we read verse 6 and verse 14 by themselves, our minds gravitate toward a singular purpose in salvation and not the dual purpose that God actually has for it. He brought Israel out that He might bring them in. That was the dual purpose that God had in saving the nation—not just to save them from Egypt, but to take them into the Promised Land of blessing.

Chapters 3 and 4 are spent exhorting the New Testament believer to NOT FOLLOW THEIR EXAMPLE OF TRUSTING GOD TO BRING THEM OUT BUT NOT TRUSTING HIM TO BRING THEM IN.

God is telling us that believing in Jesus to save us from hell but not trusting Him to take us into the abundant life is to fall short of the kind of faith and trust in our great High Priest that HE is calling us to exercise and enjoy.

He is saying that to enjoy the second rest of the abundant life that Jesus came to give, we must daily keep our eyes on our calling in

Him and the capability that He has to bring to complete fulfillment of His plans for good (Jeremiah 29:11; Romans 8:28).

In our lives, we will only obtain His best for our lives "if we hold the beginning of our confidence steadfast unto the end." It is possible for us, like Israel, to be saved from one thing but not another. It is possible for us, like Israel, to receive part of God's benefit through Christ while missing out on the Second Rest that is available to us through Him. The verses are not really teaching that you will lose your salvation, after obtaining it, if for some reason you decide to walk away later in unbelief. Israel did not lose the first portion of what God sent Moses to accomplish. They were saved from Egypt. They did not go back to Egypt and become slaves there again, but they did lose out on the second benefit that God had in mind for them when He brought them out of Egypt. The only way for them to have obtained the Second Rest was to continue on in faith when it came to trusting God to bring them INTO the PROMISED LAND. That is where they faltered, and that is what the Scripture is warning us to avoid, so we can enjoy the full benefit of God's good plan for our lives.

There are other verses that cause some people to think that salvation can be lost, but these are some of the most often cited. To keep this study somewhat short, I have limited this section to these examples. My prayer is that the explanations for these prominent passages may also serve to assuage the concern over the ones not covered herein.

CHAPTER 12

Five Things That Must Happen for a Saved Man to Lose His Salvation

For a saved man to lose his salvation, all of which are impossible:

1. Someone MUST BREAK THE SEAL OF GOD'S OWNERSHIP upon our lives.

   > And grieve not the holy Spirit of God, whereby ye are sealed unto the day of redemption. (Ephesians 4:30)

   The seal of Rome was placed upon the tomb of Jesus Christ, and it took someone far more powerful than Rome to break that seal and let Jesus out of that tomb. But who is more powerful than God? Who can break His seal of ownership and authority over the life of a child of God?

   > What? Know Ye Not that Your Body is the Temple of the Holy Ghost, which Ye Have of God, and Ye Are not your own, For Ye Are Bought with a Price..." "the Precious Blood of Christ as of a Lamb without Blemish or Spot." (1 Corinthians 6:19–20; 1 Peter 1:18–19)

You belong to God if you are saved, and He has set a permanent seal of ownership on you. No one CAN break that seal.

2.   Someone must CAST OUT the Holy Spirit.

> And because ye are sons, God hath sent forth the Spirit of his Son into your hearts, crying, Abba, Father. (Galatians 4:6)

Jesus said that when a strong man kept his house, his goods were safe in his keeping, but when a stronger than he came along and overcame him, then the stronger man would spoil his goods.

If the child of God BELONGS to JESUS, because He purchased us with His own blood (Acts 20:28), JUST WHO CAN come along and overcome Him to spoil His goods? WHO WILL CAST OUT the SPIRIT of God's Son? WHO CAN? No one can!

3.   Someone must PLUCK YOU OUT of the HAND of God.

> My sheep hear my voice, and I know them, and they follow me:
> And I give unto them eternal life; and they shall never perish, neither shall any man pluck them out of my hand.
> My Father, which gave them me, is greater than all; and no man is able to pluck them out of my Father's hand.
> I and my Father are one. (John 10:27–30)

The real question is: Are you TRULY one of HIS SHEEP? If you are, HE has ALREADY GIVEN YOU ETERNAL LIFE! In case you didn't understand what that means, HE says you will NEVER PERISH.

Remember John 3:16? He tells us that no man is ABLE to pry back the omnipotent fingers of the hand of God and remove us from the safety of His hand.

I read about a tsunami that came upon a vacation resort area a few years ago, and read the testimony of a mother whose little child was literally pulled out of her grasping hands as the force of the mighty wave came by and TOOK HER OWN BELOVED CHILD AWAY FROM HER.

She desperately wanted to be able to hold the child safely in her hands, but the wave was stronger than she was, and the child was pulled away from her to his death. This CANNOT happen to the child of God. We are secure in His and His Father's omnipotent hands.

4.   Someone MUST SEPARATE YOU FROM THE LOVE OF CHRIST.

> Who shall separate us from the love of Christ? Shall tribulation, or distress, or persecution, or famine, or nakedness, or peril, or sword?
>
> As it is written, For thy sake we are killed all the day long; we are accounted as sheep for the slaughter.
>
> Nay, in all these things we are more than conquerors through Him that loved us.
>
> For I am persuaded, that neither death, nor life, nor angels, nor principalities, nor powers, nor things present, nor things to come, Nor height, nor depth, nor any other creature, shall be able to separate us from the love of God, which is in Christ Jesus our Lord. (Romans 8:35–39)

Greater love hath no man than this, that a man LAY DOWN HIS LIFE for his friends (John 15:13). I will NEVER LEAVE THEE, nor forsake thee (Hebrews 13:5). He that cometh unto Me I will in NO WISE CAST OUT (John 6:37). Nothing and no one can separate us from His matchless love. HALLELUJAH!

5. Someone MUST TAKE YOUR NAME OUT OF THE BOOK OF LIFE.

> And whosoever was not found written in
> the book of life was cast into the lake of fire.
> (Revelation 20:15)

Only God could take your name out of the Book of Life, BUT He promises that His sheep will NEVER PERISH or be CAST OUT or FORSAKEN EVER! He says that if we come to Him, He will in no wise cast us out. The question is: Have we come to Him the way the Bible commands us to—through repentance toward God and faith in His gospel message alone?

CHAPTER 13

The Conclusion of the Whole Matter

In the final analysis, it seems to me, after much prayer and study, that salvation is a GIFT purchased by God's Son and given by the means of His mercy and grace to anyone and everyone who will meet the simple condition of receiving from God's hand the gifts of faith and repentance.

Repentance that is directed toward God acknowledges that God's ways and thoughts are higher than man's, turns away from our own rebellion against His ways and thoughts, and turns toward God again at the heart level by means of faith in the gospel message of the one-time offering for sin that Jesus Christ offered to the Father for us once and for all to provide forgiveness and to sanctify us forever in Himself.

Since salvation is a GIFT, it is not dependent on works of righteousness, which we have done, or sacramental rituals, in which we have participated. Rather, it is solely dependent upon the payment of His own precious blood as being sufficient and acceptable to the Father to assuage His terrible wrath, pay the wage of our sin (which is death), and wash our sin-stained soul white as snow.

Salvation is a gift that is given INSTANTANEOUSLY IN TIME. It is NOT A PROCESS. It is eternal in nature, which means that once the gift has been given and received, it remains the property of the receiver by the express will of the purchaser. It can neither be relinquished by the receiver nor rescinded by the giver. It is, by the giver's own testimony, everlasting, so it will last forever. It is an inheritance that will not fade away like a pipe dream or become corrupted or defiled but is reserved in the heavens for the receivers, who are saved and kept by the power of God.

I would exhort every reader to make as certain as you can that you have genuinely been born again, so you may be ready for that glorious day when the saints hear the words, "Well done, thou good and faithful servant. Enter thou into the joy of thy Lord."

Paul says, "Examine Yourselves, whether ye be in the faith; prove your own selves." (2 Corinthians 13:5)

If you have any doubts or questions still, go back and read the first three studies again, and prayerfully read the last two pages of this study, and make sure you have done what the Scriptures have told us to do.

ABOUT THE AUTHOR

My name is Jacob Higgs, and I am just a simple man who answered the call God put on me. I used to be on drugs and was nowhere close to Christ, but that all changed in 2007. In 2007, I went to a faith-based rehabilitation to get off drugs and received so much more. I received forgiveness and accepted God Almighty as my Father, all because Christ died once to pay for my sin debt. In 2013, my pastor, Jerry Mercer, presented me the opportunity to preach my first sermon. Little did he or I know that it would change the course of my Christian walk and service. Today, I am still drug-free, still sharing the gospel message, and I have a grown daughter and a lovely wife who does more for me than she will ever know. My wife, Jeannine, is a daily reminder of the unconditional love that only comes from the love of Jesus Christ.

9 7 9 8 8 9 5 2 6 2 5 4 2